64 Ways to Practice Nonviolence

Common Peace,
Center for the Advancement of Nonviolence

64 Ways to Practice Nonviolence

Curriculum and Resource Guide

SECOND EDITION

EISHA MASON
AND
PEGGY DOBREER

pro·ed
An International Publisher

8700 Shoal Creek Boulevard
Austin, Texas 78757-6897
800/897-3202 Fax 800/397-7633
www.proedinc.com

Published by: PRO-ED, Inc.
8700 Shoal Creek Boulevard
Austin, Texas 78757-6897
800/897-3202   Fax 800/397-7633
www.proedinc.com

This book was developed by Common Peace, Center for the Advancement of Nonviolence in cooperation with the publisher, PRO-ED, Inc.

ISBN-13: 978-1-4164-0359-3

Printed in the United States of America

1   2   3   4   5   6   7   8   9   10   17   16   15   14   13   12   11   10   09   08

Cover design: Trish Weber Hall

This book is dedicated to the lives of Mahatma Gandhi and Martin Luther King, Jr., and to Arun and Sunanda Gandhi, Barbara Fields, and Rev. Dr. Michael Bernard Beckwith, whose vision inspired and birthed our original form, A Season for Nonviolence, Los Angeles, and to the many individuals and Common Peace volunteers who embodied love, and infused this work with passion, patience, and persistence from inception to completion. To those who carried this vision to its fruition, and to those individuals, teachers, educators, and parents who will carry it forward, a sincere, humble, and heartfelt Thank you!

CONTENTS

RESOURCES

FOREWORD

by Arun Gandhi

My grandfather was Mohandas K. Gandhi, the renowned leader of India's nonviolent movement for independence.

In 1946, I lived with my grandfather. It was then that he taught me a lesson that led to my understanding of the meaning of my life and my personal role in creating a society of peace and harmony.

This was what might be called a double-edged lesson, or a two-in-one lesson plan. It was so simple that even I, a not-so-bright 12 year old, was able to manage it. It only required commitment and honesty, ingredients inherent in all of us.

The first part of the lesson is to ask yourself every night before going to bed: "Did I do or say anything today that hurt someone directly or indirectly?" The important thing is to answer the question honestly. To lie would only cause more hurt to oneself and others.

The next step is to figure out how you caused that hurt and put it down on a tree of violence.

On a wall in my room was a large paper on which a genealogical tree of "violence" took shape. Violence was the grandparent with two children: Physical and Passive. Physical violence used physical force against another: murder, war, beating, rape, and so on. Passive violence was without physical force but nevertheless resulted in someone being hurt: teasing, name-calling, wasting resources so that others must live in poverty, insensitivity to the suffering of others, rudeness, etc.

By analyzing myself everyday and building on this tree, I began to recognize the many faces of violence and how much I myself contributed to it.

I learned to recognize the connection between passive and physical violence. When we as individuals or society commit passive violence, whether conscious or unconscious, it breeds anger and despair in the victim that may often elicit more physical violence.

Passive violence becomes the match that ignites physical violence. If we continue to pour gasoline on flames, the fire will go on raging. We need to pour the water of "nonviolence" on to the flames, to put out the fire.

How do we recognize the waters of "nonviolence" and how do we administer them in our lives, relationships and communities?

This book, *64 Ways to Practice Nonviolence: Curriculum and Resource Guide,* offers 64 lessons that teach the skills and values that build a practice of nonviolence for young and old alike. It introduces the heroes, heroines and victories of nonviolent history. It invites us to compare violent and nonviolent responses to life's challenges. It shows us how to create positive responses in ourselves and others, like respect, understanding, compassion, and cooperation. I am delighted to introduce you to *64 Ways to Practice Nonviolence.*

You may ask, "Why 64 ways? Why not sixty-five or seventy?" There is a significant reason for this. Mohandas Gandhi, my grandfather, was assassinated on January 30, 1948, and Dr. Martin Luther

King, Jr. was assassinated on April 4, 1968. Their death dates are exactly 64 days apart. To commemorate the lives of these two great nonviolent peacemakers of the 20th century, the *Season for Nonviolence* was launched in 1998 by linking the 50th memorial anniversary of my grandfather, and the 30th memorial anniversary of Dr. King.

Out of the *Season for Nonviolence*, Common Peace, Center for the Advancement of Nonviolence was born. For the first Season, Common Peace developed the *64 Ways to Practice Nonviolence* poster. A year later, the poster began to blossom into this curriculum guide in order to make these principles of nonviolence an available course of study and character education for our children.

Because this book gives you 64 ways, it does not mean there are only 64 ways to practice peace. As you master these 64 ways you will surely discover the many more ways in which we all can work together and individually, for peace and harmony in the world. Good luck!

ARUN GANDHI
Co-Founder and President, M. K. Gandhi Institute for Nonviolence
211 Interfaith Chapel
University of Rochester
Rochester NY 14627-0423
Ph. (585) 276-3787
Fax (585) 276-2425

DEVELOPMENT

Eisha Mason Editor in Chief

Peggy Dobreer Senior Editor

EDITORIAL

Aricia Lee

Candace Carnicelli

Ana Hays

Laura Lionello

GRAPHIC DESIGN

Barry Selby Production 2006-7

Trish Weber Creative Director

Betty Mallorca Design Director

William Leidenthal Designer

Taylor Barnes Production

CONTRIBUTORS

Susanna Barkataki

Candace Carnicelli

Wanchen Chang

Owen Findley

Lisa French

Michal Golan

Michael Haggood

Bill Judson

Jelani

Eileen Latham

Etta Mason

Jaana Pekkanen

Robyn Rice

Laurie Schur

Jessica Seiden

Diane Simons

Deborah Silverman

Karen Sterling

Karen Sugerman

STANDARDS CONSULTANTS

Melissa M. Aul

Harriet Wallace

Linda Watts

***64 WAYS* POSTER 2000**

Gabriela Davis Translation

Deborah Lemon

Lorena Mendez

Trish Weber Graphics

ORIGINAL *64 WAYS* POSTER

Nick Arandes

Crystal Cheryl Bell

Michal Golan

Jennifer Hadley

Kathy Juliene

Eisha Mason

Isaiah McGee

David Silverstein

Lisa Tate Graphics

ACKNOWLEDGMENTS

A beautiful idea is just the beginning of what is required to bring that idea to fruition. Creation requires action as well as vision, discipline, creativity, cooperation, commitment, time, sweat, patience, determination, and love. This last quality—love—is so important because love is the power that sustains us through the various stages of the creative process. When we are tired and over-whelmed, when we face the unknown and patience is short, love is the critical factor that transforms work into joy!

We are so fortunate to be working with individuals who embody love and infuse this work with passion and the many special virtues that were needed to complete this curriculum guide. To those who carried this vision to its fruition, thank you!

Eisha Mason
Founder,
Common Peace, Center for the Advancement of Nonviolence

COMMON PEACE, CENTER FOR THE ADVANCEMENT OF NONVIOLENCE MISSION STATEMENT

To heal, empower, and revitalize our lives and
our communities through the practice of nonviolence as a way of life.

Through education, inspiration, and cooperative
action, we are creating a society that honors the
dignity and worth of every human being.

We believe that each person can move
the world in the direction of peace through their
daily nonviolent choice and action.

INTRODUCTION TO NONVIOLENCE EDUCATION

When Common Peace, Center for the Advancement of Nonviolence invites an audience to share their responses to the question, "What is violence and where did you learn about it?" responses abound; everyone has something powerful and poignant to share. However, when we ask, "What is nonviolence and where did you learn about it?," responses are far fewer, ambivalent, sometimes conflicted; sometimes there is only the most brief and superficial response. Most people sense that there must be another way. However, because nonviolence is not part of their culture, internal paradigm, or vocabulary, it is more challenging to envision and articulate. They may have a few images that inspire them, or names and stories of people who demonstrated nonviolent ways in history, but for the most part, the concept of nonviolence is loaded with misperceptions, ready judgments and myths.

So how can we now move toward a more peaceful world, society, community, school, classroom, home, life, and self, if we don't know how? We do so by developing a language, dialogue, exploration, stories and history of nonviolence, new values, principles to live by, habits to practice, and new agreements. *64 Ways to Practice Nonviolence* seeks to equip its readers with the tools to facilitate this shift in our personal and social culture. Our mission is to demonstrate that there is another code of conduct. There are principles for living, and values that can guide one's life and choices other than those we take for granted everyday through our predominant culture's violence. Our intention is to make information and awareness about nonviolence as accessible and common, and as normal and "natural" as information about violence in today's society. This system, or culture of nonviolence, based on a reverence for life, is powerful and effective. It is a viable alternative to systems based on inequality, domination, injustice, violence, punishment, and revenge.

The *64 Ways to Practice Nonviolence* curriculum is designed to facilitate the exploration of a way of life known as nonviolence. As your community undertakes this journey, participants will debate challenging questions, and many times they may not arrive at a neat and clear resolution of the issues at hand. Many times, as the facilitator, you will be asked questions about the practice of nonviolence and feel you do not have the "perfect" answer.

Keep in mind that nonviolence challenges our traditional ways of seeing and thinking. For the first time, many of us will be seeking answers outside the boundaries of our cultural norms and traditions. This may be our first awareness that what we have always accepted is not carved in stone. This may be the first time we seriously consider that there are other possibilities that we have barely dreamed of, other choices we have not considered. At times, this exploration may feel uncomfortable. However, this questioning process is the first step toward change.

When we begin to question what we have taken for granted—ways of thinking, being and relating, accepted approaches to solving problems, and ways of perceiving ourselves, others, and the world—there is an opportunity for something new to happen, a new insight or meaning to be revealed, or a new solution to come forth. Our mission is to challenge our social agreements, provoke questioning, encourage dialogue, and inspire new creative solutions.

Our purpose is to illustrate that there are many great souls—some famous and some not so famous—who have lived by this alternative code, worked to alter the course of violence, and thereby changed the world significantly. Each of us, and each one of our students, is a potential hero of nonviolence.

We are committed to creating safe spaces in which we can wrestle with life changing questions, explore new ways of thinking and being, and experiment with the practice of nonviolence. That is the purpose of the *64 Ways to Practice Nonviolence* poster and curriculum as well as with Common Peace, Center for the Advancement of Nonviolence trainings, workshops, forums, and special events. We are continuing to develop more tools and to create more experiences in which we can grow together.

To this latest edition of the curriculum, we have added more resources, including an expanded glossary, bibliography, and a new "How to Use the Curriculum Guide" with Academic Standards, with more Study Aid Worksheets to further guide both teachers and students through this process. As a way to provide that vision of our shared future, we have also added to our name, Common Peace, for we must keep that vision before us in a language we can all understand and to which we can all respond. Common Peace is the touchstone that continually brings us into the present, and calls us forward. What we know of nonviolence is that it is both an everyday practice and a strategy for change. It is both the foundation and the goal. Our hope is that Common Peace causes people to reflect on what all people share in common—common needs, hopes and dreams, common sense, common ground, a common humanity, and a common source. Let us create a common peace!

With all of the testing, standards, and separate school districts' requirements, it can seem like there is no time to add "one more thing" to a teacher's schedule. Yet, how can we not make time for peace? What in truth could be more essential to teaching than creating a safe space, nurturing self-esteem, fostering social skills and mutual respect in a world that is ever more diverse? With the aid of the academic standards, we trust teachers and youth workers will integrate this curriculum into their classrooms and reap the rewards. In support of our ongoing efforts to improve and update the curriculum, we look forward to hearing about the experiences, challenges, stories and victories this curriculum brings into being, as well as any further ideas to expand upon this work of common peace in our time.

Our vision is to empower every individual to "be the change you want to see."—Gandhi

64 Ways
TO PRACTICE NONVIOLENCE
Second Edition

GUIDELINES AND AIDS
FOR CURRICULUM USE

This section outlines the elements and
cross-references provided in this workbook.

◆

It includes a standards assessment chart for
California's language arts requirements, with
grade level and discipline area recommendations.

◆

It also includes vocabulary development
and literary response worksheets for use
in the classroom.

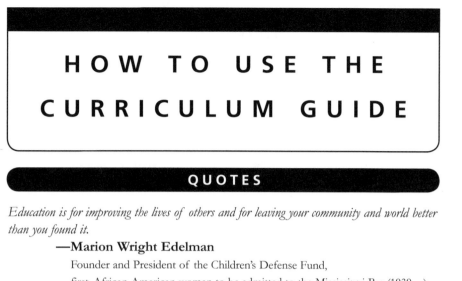

HOW TO USE THE CURRICULUM GUIDE

QUOTES

Education is for improving the lives of others and for leaving your community and world better than you found it.

—Marion Wright Edelman
> Founder and President of the Children's Defense Fund,
> first African American woman to be admitted to the Mississippi Bar (1939—)

Education is not the filling of a pail, but the lighting of a fire.

—William Butler Yeats
> Leader of the Irish Literary Renaissance (1865-1939)

HOW TO APPROACH THIS CURRICULUM

The *64 Ways to Practice Nonviolence Curriculum Guide* provides a complete standard specific language arts model for middle and high school students, a thorough use of arts and theatre to encourage personal expression, and an *in-depth* approach to values clarification and character development.

Whether introduced in an individual classroom, a youth group, a school, or district-wide campaign, the *64 Ways* curriculum provides a means for building communities that honor the dignity and worth of every person. The history and practices shared in this book demonstrate the efficacy of nonviolence as a way of life that works.

HOW TO USE THIS CURRICULUM GUIDE

This curriculum is designed to be highly flexible and adaptable. The facilitator/teacher is encouraged to thoroughly read the *Core Concepts* of the curriculum and to become familiar with the *64 Ways*. After doing so, we suggest the teacher/facilitator then allow the requirements of the setting, and their own practice of nonviolence and sense of creativity guide the course of study.

Following are some simple organizing elements of this curriculum that will assist you in adapting the *64 Ways* material to a format most ideal for your community.

continued ▶

HOW TO USE THIS CURRICULUM GUIDE, *continued*

ACADEMIC STANDARDS

- A grid is provided to indicate the grade level and language arts standards covered in each piece of the curriculum.
- The Standards Guide also provides direction to curriculum provided for additional discipline areas including: research, social science, art, theatre arts, experiential activities for community building, life science, and math.
- Study Aid Worksheets are provided for Vocabulary and Literary Response homework or classwork.

INTRODUCTORY CONCEPTS

- The Historical Perspective section at the front of the book relates to the Nobel Peace Laureates for a Decade Dedicated to a Culture of Peace and Nonviolence for The Children of the World.
- It reviews the nonviolence principles of Gandhi, King, and Common Peace, Center for the Advancement of Nonviolence.
- The Four Core Concepts Section provides material for introductory lessons on nonviolence. This material should be reviewed before beginning the *64 Ways*, to provide a context and vocabulary for the inquiry.

64 WAYS FORMAT

- Each of the *64 Ways* is represented by its own chapter. The first 23 ways of the *64 Ways* curriculum suggest ways in which to address the practice of nonviolence with oneself. Days 24 – 46 address ways to practice nonviolence in interpersonal relationships; days 47 – 64 address the practice of nonviolence in community and society.

- The box at the beginning of each chapter contains the practice of the day and message from the original *64 Ways to Practice Nonviolence* poster.

- The inspirational quotes can be paired with the activity you choose and the maturity level of the students. A "literary response worksheet" for homework or classroom assignments is provided on page xxxi.

- The discussion questions are provided to deepen the exploration and dialogue. Again, questions are designed for the varying maturity level of students. We recommend several ways of using them and invite your suggestions regarding other ways:

    1) Language arts classes may use quotes as a journaling tool.

    2) Social Science classes may want to organize panel discussions, rotating the students on the panel, and allowing the remaining students to respond to the panel orally or in a written homework response.

    3) Smaller classes or groups may want to "sit in council" to address a question. In council, a symbolic item is used as a talking piece (a favorite stone or shell). It is passed clockwise around the circle. Only the person holding the talking piece may speak. There is no cross-talk in the circle. Each person is asked to speak "leanly," from the heart, and to listen deeply with respect as others share their views. Speaking without planning ahead allows full attention on the circle.

    By sitting in a circle, the students realize equity and shared value in the ideas expressed. A communal voice can often be discerned. The teacher is present to point to that voice and keep the group focused, safe, and on topic, but not to impose his or her personal views on the group (Zimmerman, 1999). For further information on this method, visit http://www.ojaifoundation.org.

continued ▶

HOW TO USE THIS CURRICULUM GUIDE, *continued*

4) Art classes may express their responses through drawing, painting, collage, poetry, theatre, or developing cartoons.

- Each curriculum activity is represented by a picture icon that designates a field of study or type of activity. There is an icon legend provided with the standards chart on page xvi.

- Service Learning is an integral component of this curriculum, particularly in the section on community practices, as students expand their awareness of responsibility in community.

CURRICULUM GOALS

As you review these materials, keep in mind our goals to:

- Improve language arts scores and comprehension by providing, as Dr. Martin Luther King wrote, "worthy objectives on which to concentrate."
- Develop critical thinking skills, and written and oral communication skills.
- Inspire and empower civic participation and increase competency in civics and social studies.
- Challenge violent cultural norms.
- Create safe spaces for challenging old ideas, exploring new ways of being, and experimenting with the practice of nonviolence.
- Provoke creative questions and facilitate thought, reflection, and dialogue.

Building a conscience is what discipline is all about. The goal is for a youngster to end up believing in decency, and acting, whether anyone is watching or not, in helpful and kind and generous, thoughtful ways. (1996)
> — **James L. Hymes, Jr.**
> U.S. Child Development Specialist, author of
> *A Sensible Approach to Discipline*

LIST OF 64 WAYS TO PRACTICE NONVIOLENCE

ICON LEGEND AND LANGUAGE STANDARDS ALIGNMENT CHART

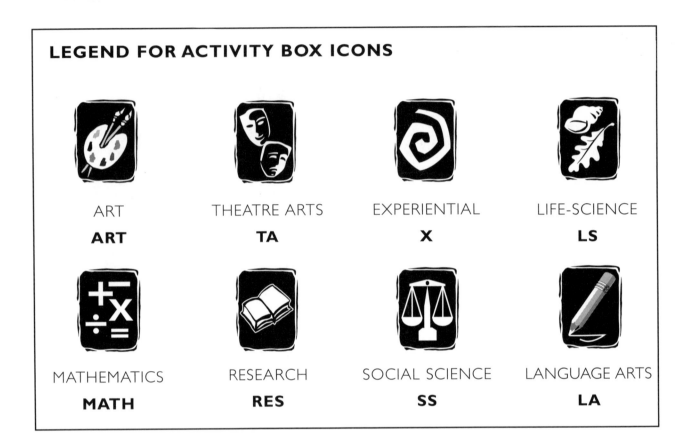

LEGEND FOR ACTIVITY BOX ICONS

ART	THEATRE ARTS	EXPERIENTIAL	LIFE-SCIENCE
ART	**TA**	**X**	**LS**
MATHEMATICS	RESEARCH	SOCIAL SCIENCE	LANGUAGE ARTS
MATH	**RES**	**SS**	**LA**

ALIGNING THE 64 WAYS ACTIVITIES WITH READING AND WRITING STANDARDS

The reading comprehension skills and writing applications across the top of the standards chart beginning on the next page are based on the California State Standards for Reading and Language Arts. California is a leader in creating comprehensive state standards for addressing essential skills. While there are no current National Educational Standards, most state standards have been based on these skills and applications below.

The abbreviation at the beginning of each activity corresponds to the icons above. The icon describes the course of study and discipline area for which the exercise was developed. Although many disciplines overlap and are interchangeable in the classroom, this information will help to guide your use of the *64 Ways* activities in particular aspects of the course work being addressed, and will guide you through the skill levels and grade levels of the students. All of the exercises may be adjusted or adapted for use in many environments.

Keep in mind that each chapter is an in-depth vocabulary lesson and each quote provided for discussion applies critical thinking and literary response skills. Worksheets are provided in this section, which may be copied for class and homework assignments.

ICON	No.	GL	OD	R1	R2	R3	R4	R5	R6	R7	R8	W1	W2	W3	W4	W5	W6	W7	W8	W9	W10
1. CULTURE																					
ART	C1.1	6-8	√	√		√	√	√		√		√	√		√					√	√
ART	C1.2	9-12	√	√	√	√	√	√	√	√		√	√		√	√		√		√	√
ART	C1.3	9-12	√	√		√	√	√		√	√	√	√	√	√	√		√		√	√
ART	C1.4	10-12	√	√		√	√	√	√	√	√	√	√	√	√					√	√
LA	C1.5	6-9	√	√	√	√	√	√	√	√	√	√	√	√	√	√		√		√	√
LA	C1.6	10-12	√	√		√	√	√		√	√	√	√		√	√				√	√
LA	C1.7	6-9	√	√	√	√	√	√	√	√	√	√	√	√	√	√		√		√	√
LA	C1.8	6-9		√	√	√	√	√	√	√	√	√	√	√	√	√	√				
LA	C1.9	10-12	√	√			√	√	√	√		√	√	√	√	√	√	√			√
LA	C1.10	10-12	√	√			√	√	√	√	√	√	√	√	√			√	√		√
2. VIOLENCE																					
X	C2.1	6-12	√	√	√	√	√	√	√	√	√	√	√	√	√	√					√
LA	C2.2	9-12	√	√	√	√	√	√	√	√	√	√	√	√	√	√				√	√
LA	C2.3	6-9	√	√	√	√	√	√	√	√	√	√	√					√		√	√
X	C2.4	6-8	√	√	√	√	√	√	√	√	√	√	√	√	√					√	√
ART	C2.5	9-12	√	√	√	√	√	√	√	√	√	√	√	√	√	√				√	√
RES	C2.6	11-12	√	√	√	√	√	√	√	√	√	√	√	√	√	√	√			√	√
RES	C2.7	6-12	√	√	√	√	√	√	√	√	√	√	√	√	√	√	√			√	√
RES	C2.8	10-12	√	√	√	√	√	√	√	√	√	√	√	√	√	√				√	√
3. POWER																					
LA	C3.1	6-12	√	√	√	√	√	√	√	√	√	√	√	√	√	√				√	√
ART	C3.2	6-9	√	√	√	√	√	√	√	√	√	√	√	√	√	√		√		√	√
LA	C3.3	9-12	√	√	√	√	√	√	√	√	√	√	√	√	√	√				√	√
LA	C3.4	10-12	√	√	√	√	√	√	√	√	√	√	√	√	√	√	√			√	√
LA	C3.5	6-10	√	√	√	√	√	√	√	√	√	√	√	√	√	√				√	√
X	C3.6	6-12	√	√	√	√	√	√	√	√	√	√	√	√	√	√		√			√
X	C3.7	11-12	√	√	√	√	√	√	√	√	√	√	√	√	√	√	√				√
LA	C3.8	6-9	√	√	√	√	√	√	√	√	√	√	√	√	√	√	√	√			√
RES	C3.9	10-12	√	√	√	√	√	√	√	√	√	√	√	√	√	√			√	√	√
RES	C3.10	9-12	√	√	√	√	√	√	√	√	√	√	√	√	√	√	√				√
3. NONVIOLENCE																					
LA	C4.1	6-9	√	√	√	√	√	√	√	√	√	√	√	√	√	√		√			√
ART	C4.2	6-12	√	√	√	√	√	√	√	√	√	√	√	√	√	√		√		√	√
X	C4.3	6-8	√	√	√	√	√	√	√	√	√	√	√	√	√	√				√	√
TA	C4.4	10-12	√	√	√	√	√	√	√	√	√	√	√	√	√	√	√	√		√	√
LA	C4.5	6-12	√	√		√	√	√	√	√	√	√	√		√	√				√	√
LA	C4.6	6-12	√	√	√	√	√	√	√	√	√	√	√	√	√	√		√			√
X	C4.7	10-12	√	√	√	√	√	√	√	√	√	√	√	√	√	√	√				√
LA	C4.8	8-10	√	√	√	√	√	√	√	√	√	√	√	√	√	√			√		√

Column key: OD = Developing Oral Comm.; R1 = Point of View; R2 = Fact from Opinion; R3 = Drawing Conclusions; R4 = Interpret Events & Abstract; R5 = Use Context Clues; R6 = Understand Cause & Effect; R7 = Understand Main Idea; R8 = Compare & Contrast; W1 = Narrative; W2 = Descriptive; W3 = Persuasive; W4 = Expository; W5 = Res. & Application; W6 = Lit. Response; W7 = Poetry/Prose; W8 = Letter Writing; W9 = Journal Record Keeping; W10 = Language Mechanics

ICON	No.	GL	OD	R1	R2	R3	R4	R5	R6	R7	R8	W1	W2	W3	W4	W5	W6	W7	W8	W9	W10
DAY 1 COURAGE																					
LA	1.1	6-12	√	√		√	√	√		√		√	√		√					√	√
LA	1.2	6-12	√	√	√	√	√	√	√	√		√	√		√	√		√		√	√
LA	1.3	10-12	√	√		√	√	√		√	√	√	√	√	√	√		√		√	√
X	1.4	8-12	√	√		√	√	√	√	√	√	√	√	√	√	√				√	√
RES	1.5	9-12	√	√	√	√	√	√	√	√	√	√	√	√	√	√		√		√	√
LA	1.6	7-9	√	√	√	√	√	√	√	√	√	√			√	√				√	√
DAY 2 SMILING																					
MATH	2.1	6-7	√	√	√	√	√	√	√	√	√	√	√	√	√	√					√
X	2.2	8-10	√	√	√	√	√	√	√	√	√	√	√	√	√					√	√
X	2.3			√	√	√	√	√	√	√	√	√	√	√	√			√		√	√
LS	2.4			√	√	√	√	√	√	√	√	√	√	√	√	√				√	√
DAY 3 GRATITUDE																					
ART	3.1	6-8	√	√	√	√	√	√	√	√	√	√	√	√	√	√				√	√
LA	3.2	6-12	√	√	√	√	√	√	√	√	√	√	√	√	√	√	√			√	√
ART	3.3	6-12	√	√	√	√	√	√	√	√	√	√	√	√	√	√	√			√	√
LA	3.4	6-12	√	√	√	√	√	√	√	√	√	√	√	√	√	√				√	√
DAY 4 CARING																					
LS	4.1	10-12	√	√	√	√	√	√	√	√	√	√	√	√	√	√		√		√	√
X	4.2	6-9	√	√	√	√	√	√	√	√	√	√	√	√	√	√				√	√
X	4.3	6-7	√	√	√	√	√	√	√	√	√	√	√	√	√	√	√			√	√
X	4.4	6-9	√	√	√	√	√	√	√	√	√	√	√	√	√	√				√	√
DAY 5 BELIEVING																					
TA	5.1	6-12	√	√	√	√	√	√	√	√	√	√	√	√	√	√	√	√			√
X	5.2	6-12	√	√	√	√	√	√	√	√	√	√	√	√	√	√				√	√
LA	5.3	11-12	√	√	√	√	√	√	√	√	√	√	√	√	√	√	√				√
RES	5.4	8-12	√	√	√	√	√	√	√	√	√	√	√	√	√	√			√		√
ART	5.5	6-9	√	√	√	√	√	√	√	√	√	√	√	√	√			√		√	√
LS	5.6	6-9	√	√	√	√	√	√	√	√	√	√	√	√	√			√		√	√
DAY 6 SIMPLICITY																					
TA	6.1	6-10	√	√	√	√	√	√	√	√	√				√						
RES	6.2	10-12	√	√	√	√	√	√	√	√	√				√	√				√	√
X	6.3	6-12	√	√		√		√							√						
X	6.4	6-9	√			√		√		√					√						
RES	6.5	6-8		√	√	√	√	√	√	√	√				√	√	√				√

ICON	No.	GL	OD	R1	R2	R3	R4	R5	R6	R7	R8	W1	W2	W3	W4	W5	W6	W7	W8	W9	W10
DAY 7 EDUCATION																					
X	7.1	6-12	√	√	√	√	√	√	√	√	√	√	√	√	√	√	√	√		√	√
LA	7.2	6-12	√	√		√	√	√	√	√	√	√	√	√	√	√				√	√
ART	7.3	10-12	√	√	√	√	√	√	√	√	√	√	√		√						√
SS	7.4	6-8	√	√		√	√	√	√	√	√										√
SS	7.5	8-12	√	√	√	√	√	√	√	√	√										√
RES	7.6	9-12		√	√	√	√	√	√	√	√					√	√	√		√	√
DAY 8 HEALING																					
ART	8.1	11-12		√	√	√	√	√	√	√	√										
X	8.2	9-12	√		√	√	√	√	√	√		√	√								√
RES	8.3	9-12	√	√	√	√	√	√	√	√	√	√	√	√	√	√	√	√	√		√
X	8.4	9-12	√	√	√	√	√	√	√	√	√	√		√	√						√
DAY 9 DREAMING																					
LA	9.1	10-12		√	√	√	√	√	√	√											
ART	9.2	11-12	√	√	√	√	√	√	√	√	√	√	√	√	√	√	√				√
LA	9.3	6-8	√	√		√	√	√	√	√											√
LA	9.4	11-12	√	√	√	√	√	√	√	√	√	√		√		√	√	√			√
DAY 10 FAITH																					
ART	10.1	6-12		√			√		√					√							√
RES	10.2	6-12	√	√	√	√	√	√	√	√	√		√	√	√	√	√				
LA	10.3	11-12	√	√	√	√	√	√	√	√	√	√	√		√		√	√	√	√	√
LA	0.4	6-12	√	√	√	√	√	√	√	√		√	√				√				√
DAY 11 CONTEMPLATION																					
X	11.1	6-12	√	√			√														
SCI	11.2	6-12			√	√															
X	11.3	6-12			√	√															
X	11.4	6-12		√		√		√	√		√	√					√				√
ART	11.5	6-12			√	√		√	√		√					√					
LA	11.6	6-12		√	√	√	√		√			√		√		√	√			√	√
DAY 12 DISCIPLINE																					
X	12.1	6-8	√	√		√			√	√										√	√
X	12.2	10-12	√	√	√	√	√	√	√	√	√		√							√	√
RES	12.3	6-12	√	√	√	√	√	√	√	√		√	√	√	√	√				√	√
DAY 13 CREATIVITY																					
ART	12.1	6-12		√		√	√	√		√			√		√						√
ART	12.2	6-12	√	√	√	√	√	√	√	√	√	√	√	√	√	√		√		√	√
LA	12.3	6-12	√	√	√	√	√	√	√	√	√	√	√		√			√			√
LA	12.4	8-10	√			√	√		√	√		√	√		√						√
ART	12.5	6-12		√		√		√	√	√	√		√	√		√	√	√			√

ICON	No.	GL	OD	R1	R2	R3	R4	R5	R6	R7	R8	W1	W2	W3	W4	W5	W6	W7	W8	W9	W10
DAY 14 HUMILITY																					
LA	14.1	6-12	√	√		√	√	√		√		√	√								
TA	14.2	10-12	√	√	√	√	√	√	√	√		√	√								
RES	14.3	6-8	√	√		√	√	√		√		√	√		√	√					√
ART	14.4	8-10	√	√		√	√	√	√	√	√	√	√	√	√	√					√
SS	14.5	6-7	√	√		√	√	√	√	√		√	√	√	√						√
DAY 15 REVERENCE																					
ART	15.1	6-9	√	√	√	√	√	√	√	√	√	√	√		√					√	
LA	15.2	6-12	√	√	√	√	√	√	√	√	√	√	√		√	√		√		√	√
ART	15.3	9-12	√	√	√	√	√	√	√	√	√		√	√	√	√		√		√	√
X	15.4	6-12	√	√		√	√	√	√	√	√	√	√							√	
LA	15.5	6-12	√	√	√	√	√	√	√	√	√	√	√	√	√			√	√	√	√
X	15.6	6-12	√	√	√	√	√	√	√	√	√	√	√	√	√	√					
RES	15.7	10-12	√	√	√	√	√	√	√	√	√	√	√	√	√	√	√			√	
DAY 16 LEADERSHIP																					
TA	16.1	10-12	√	√	√	√	√	√	√	√	√	√	√	√	√	√					√
LA	16.1	11-12	√	√	√	√	√	√	√	√	√	√	√	√	√	√		√			√
LA	16.1	10-12	√	√	√	√	√	√	√	√	√	√	√	√							√
RES	16.1	10-12	√	√	√	√	√	√	√	√	√	√	√	√	√	√	√				
TA	16.1	10-12	√	√	√	√	√	√	√	√	√	√	√	√	√	√	√				
DAY 17 INTEGRITY																					
ART	17.1	9-12	√	√	√	√	√	√	√	√	√	√	√		√	√					
LA	17.2	6-9	√	√	√	√	√	√	√	√	√	√	√		√	√					√
LA	17.3	6-10	√	√	√	√	√	√	√	√	√	√	√		√						√
X	17.4	10-12	√	√	√	√	√	√	√	√	√	√	√		√	√					
DAY 18 FREEDOM																					
ART	18.1	6-12	√	√		√	√	√	√	√		√	√	√	√	√		√			√
RES	18.2	11-12	√	√	√	√	√	√	√	√		√	√	√	√	√	√				√
SS	18.3	8-12	√	√		√	√		√	√	√	√	√	√	√						√
RES	18.4	8-12	√	√	√	√	√	√	√	√											√
LA	18.5	6-12	√																		
X	18.6	9-12	√	√		√	√	√		√	√	√	√	√	√	√				√	√
DAY 19 ACCEPTANCE																					
X	19.1	6-9	√	√	√	√	√	√	√			√	√								√
LA	19.2	6-9	√	√		√	√	√		√	√	√	√								√
LA	19.3	6-12	√	√		√	√	√		√		√	√		√						√
ART	19.4	6-12	√	√		√	√	√													√
X	19.5	6-9	√	√	√	√	√	√	√	√		√	√	√	√						√
SS	19.6	11-12	√	√	√	√	√	√	√	√	√	√	√	√	√	√					√

ICON	No.	GL	OD	R1	R2	R3	R4	R5	R6	R7	R8	W1	W2	W3	W4	W5	W6	W7	W8	W9	W10
DAY 20 SELF-FORGIVENESS																					
X	20.1	6–12	√	√		√	√	√		√		√	√	√	√	√			√		√
LA	20.2	9–12	√	√		√	√	√	√	√		√	√	√	√						
LA	20.3	10–12	√	√		√	√	√	√	√		√	√	√	√					√	√
X	20.4	6–12	√	√		√	√	√	√	√	√	√	√	√	√	√				√	√
DAY 21 INSPIRATION																					
TA	21.1	6–12	√	√		√	√	√	√	√	√	√		√							√
X	21.2	6–8	√	√		√	√	√	√	√		√	√	√	√	√	√				√
ART	21.3	6–10	√	√		√	√	√	√	√			√								√
DAY 22 MISSION																					
LA	22.1	6–12		√		√	√	√	√	√		√		√		√			√		√
ART	22.2	6–12	√	√		√	√	√		√		√		√		√	√				√
LA	22.3	6–12	√	√		√	√	√	√	√	√	√	√	√	√	√			√		√
X	22.4	8–12	√	√		√	√	√	√	√			√	√	√	√	√		√	√	√
DAY 23 PRAYER																					
RES	23.1	9–12	√	√	√	√	√	√		√	√	√	√	√	√	√	√	√			√
X	23.2	6–12	√	√		√	√	√	√	√		√	√	√	√	√	√	√			√
ART	23.3	6–12	√	√			√	√		√	√		√	√							√
LA	23.4	6–12	√	√		√	√	√	√	√		√	√	√							√
DAY 24 HARMONY																					
ART	24.1	6–9	√	√		√	√	√		√		√	√	√	√						√
LA	24.2	6–9	√	√	√	√	√	√		√		√	√	√	√	√					√
X	24.3	9–12	√	√	√	√	√	√		√	√	√	√	√	√						√
X	24.4	6–10	√	√		√	√	√	√	√	√	√	√	√	√						√
X	24.5	6–12	√	√	√	√	√	√	√	√		√	√	√	√					√	√
LA	24.6	9–12	√	√	√	√	√	√	√	√		√	√	√	√	√	√			√	√
DAY 25 FRIENDLINESS																					
X	25.1	6–9	√	√		√	√	√	√	√		√	√	√	√						
X	25.2	6–12	√	√	√	√	√	√		√	√	√	√	√	√						√
ART	25.3	6–9	√	√		√	√	√		√		√	√		√						√
ART	25.4	6–9	√	√		√	√	√		√		√	√								√
X	25.5	6–12	√	√		√	√	√	√	√	√	√	√	√	√	√					
X	25.6	9–12	√	√		√	√	√	√	√		√	√	√	√					√	√
DAY 26 RESPECT																					
ART	26.1	6–12	√	√		√	√	√		√	√		√							√	√
LA	26.2	6–12	√	√	√	√	√	√		√		√	√	√	√						√
X	26.3	7–10	√	√	√	√	√	√		√		√	√	√	√						√
X	26.4	6–12	√	√	√	√	√	√		√		√	√	√	√					√	√
TA	26.5	9–12	√	√	√	√	√	√	√	√	√	√	√	√	√	√	√	√		√	√

ICON	No.	GL	OD	R1	R2	R3	R4	R5	R6	R7	R8	W1	W2	W3	W4	W5	W6	W7	W8	W9	W10
DAY 27 GENEROSITY																					
X	27.1	6-9	√	√		√	√	√	√	√		√	√	√	√	√					√
X	27.2	6-8	√	√		√	√	√	√	√		√	√	√	√						√
MATH	27.3	9-12	√	√	√	√		√	√	√		√	√	√	√	√	√		√	√	√
RES	27.4	10-12	√	√	√	√	√	√	√	√	√	√	√	√	√	√	√				√
DAY 28 LISTENING																					
X	28.1	6-12	√	√	√	√	√	√	√	√		√	√	√	√						√
X	28.2	9-12	√	√	√	√	√	√	√	√	√	√	√	√	√					√	√
TA	28.3	8-12	√	√	√	√	√	√	√	√	√	√	√	√	√					√	√
X	28.4	10-12	√	√	√	√	√	√	√	√	√		√	√			√				√
DAY 29 FORGIVENESS																					
LS	29.1	9-12	√	√	√	√	√	√	√	√	√	√	√	√	√				√		√
SS	29.2	10-12	√	√	√	√	√	√	√	√		√	√	√	√	√					
ART	29.3	6-12	√	√	√	√	√	√	√	√		√	√	√	√					√	√
DAY 30 AMENDS																					
LA	30.1	9-12	√	√	√	√	√	√	√	√	√	√	√	√	√		√		√	√	√
TA	30.2	6-9	√	√	√	√	√	√	√	√	√	√	√	√	√	√					√
LA	30.3	6-12	√	√	√	√	√	√	√	√	√	√	√	√	√						√
RES	30.4	9-12	√	√	√	√	√	√	√	√	√	√	√	√	√		√				√
LA	30.5	10-12	√	√	√	√	√	√	√	√	√	√	√		√	√					√
DAY 31 CONFLICT RESOLUTION																					
LA	31.1	9-12	√	√	√	√	√	√	√	√	√	√	√	√	√	√				√	√
LA	31.2	6-12	√	√	√	√	√	√	√	√	√	√	√	√	√	√				√	√
X	31.3	6-9	√	√	√	√	√	√	√	√	√	√	√	√	√	√	√			√	√
RES	31.4	8-12	√	√	√	√	√	√	√	√	√	√	√	√	√	√				√	√
RES	31.5	9-12	√	√	√	√	√	√	√	√	√	√	√	√	√					√	√
X	31.6	10-12	√	√	√	√	√	√	√	√	√	√	√	√	√	√	√			√	√
DAY 32 PATIENCE																					
TA	32.1	6-12	√	√	√	√	√	√	√	√	√	√	√	√	√	√					√
LA	32.2	9-12	√	√	√	√	√	√	√	√	√	√	√	√	√					√	√
LA	32.3	9-12	√	√	√	√	√	√	√	√	√	√	√	√	√	√	√	√		√	√
DAY 33 APPRECIATION																					
ART	33.1	6-9	√	√		√	√	√	√	√		√	√	√	√	√		√		√	√
LA	33.2	6-12	√	√		√	√	√	√	√		√	√	√	√	√	√			√	√
LA	33.3	9-12	√	√	√	√	√	√	√	√	√	√	√	√	√	√	√			√	√
X	33.4	8-12	√	√	√	√	√	√	√	√		√	√	√	√						√
X	33.5	6-12	√	√	√	√	√	√	√	√		√	√	√	√						
ART	33.6	6-12	√	√	√	√	√	√	√	√		√	√	√	√			√	√		
RES	33.7	8-12	√	√	√	√	√	√	√	√	√	√	√	√	√	√			√	√	√

ICON	No.	GL	OD	R1	R2	R3	R4	R5	R6	R7	R8	W1	W2	W3	W4	W5	W6	W7	W8	W9	W10
DAY 34 LOVE																					
X	34.1	6-9	√	√		√	√	√	√	√	√	√	√	√							√
LA	34.2	9-12	√	√	√	√	√	√	√	√	√	√	√	√	√	√		√			√
TA	34.3	10-12	√	√	√	√	√	√	√	√		√	√	√	√	√		√		√	√
X	34.4	6-12	√	√	√	√	√	√	√	√	√	√	√	√	√	√					√
RES	34.5	9-12	√	√	√	√	√	√	√	√	√	√	√	√	√	√	√	√			√
LA	34.6	6-12	√	√		√	√	√	√		√	√	√	√	√						
DAY 35 UNDERSTANDING																					
ART	35.1	8-12	√	√		√	√	√	√	√	√	√	√	√	√			√		√	√
LA	35.2	6-8	√	√	√	√	√	√	√	√	√	√	√	√	√	√		√		√	√
X	35.3	9-12	√	√	√	√	√	√	√	√	√	√	√	√	√	√	√				√
TA	35.4	6-12	√	√	√	√	√	√	√	√	√	√	√	√	√	√					√
DAY 36 MINDFULNESS																					
X	36.1	6-8	√	√	√	√	√	√	√	√		√	√	√	√	√				√	√
LA	36.2	6-12	√	√	√	√	√	√	√	√	√	√	√	√	√	√		√		√	√
X	36.3	6-12	√	√	√	√	√	√	√	√	√	√	√	√	√	√				√	√
X	36.4	10-12	√	√	√	√	√	√	√	√		√	√			√	√			√	√
DAY 37 GRACIOUSNESS																					
ART	37.1	6-12	√	√		√	√	√	√	√		√	√	√	√	√					
TA	37.2	6-12	√	√	√	√	√	√	√	√	√	√	√	√	√	√	√	√			
LA	37.3	6-9	√	√	√	√	√	√	√	√	√	√	√	√	√	√				√	
DAY 38 KINDNESS																					
X	38.1	6-12	√	√	√	√	√	√	√	√	√	√	√	√	√	√	√			√	√
LA	38.2	6-9	√	√	√	√	√	√	√	√	√	√	√	√	√	√				√	√
RES	38.3	6-12	√	√	√	√	√	√	√	√	√	√	√	√	√	√	√				√
RES	38.4	6-8	√	√	√	√	√	√	√	√		√	√	√	√	√				√	√
RES	38.5	6-12	√		√	√	√	√	√	√		√	√	√	√	√					√
DAY 39 DIALOGUE																					
TA	39.1	9-12	√	√	√	√	√	√	√	√	√	√	√	√	√	√				√	√
X	39.2	6-8	√	√	√	√	√	√	√	√	√	√	√	√	√	√				√	√
X	39.3	9-12	√	√	√	√	√	√	√	√	√	√	√	√	√	√					√
X	39.4	6-12	√	√	√	√	√	√	√	√	√	√	√	√	√	√					√
X	39.5	9-12	√	√	√	√	√	√	√	√	√	√	√	√	√	√					√
TA	39.6	9-12	√	√	√	√	√	√	√	√	√	√	√	√	√	√	√				√
RES	39.7	11-12	√	√	√	√	√	√	√	√	√	√	√			√	√	√		√	√
DAY 40 UNITY																					
ART	40.1	6-8	√	√			√	√		√		√	√	√				√			√
LA	40.2	9-12	√	√	√	√	√	√	√	√	√	√	√	√	√	√	√	√			√
ART	40.3	6-12	√	√	√	√	√	√	√	√	√	√	√	√							√

ICON	No.	GL	OD	R1	R2	R3	R4	R5	R6	R7	R8	W1	W2	W3	W4	W5	W6	W7	W8	W9	W10
DAY 41 OPENNESS																					
X	41.1	6-9	√	√			√	√		√		√	√	√		√					√
X	41.2	9-12	√	√	√	√	√	√	√	√	√	√	√	√	√	√				√	√
ART	41.3	6-9	√	√																	√
LA	41.4	9-12	√	√	√	√	√	√	√	√	√	√	√	√	√	√	√	√			√
X	41.5	10-12	√	√	√	√	√	√	√	√	√	√	√	√	√	√					√
DAY 42 ACCOUNTABILITY																					
X	42.1	6-12	√	√		√	√		√	√		√	√	√	√	√				√	√
LA	42.2	6-12	√	√		√	√	√	√	√	√	√	√	√	√	√				√	√
LA	42.3	9-12	√	√	√	√	√	√	√	√	√	√	√	√	√		√	√		√	√
X	42.4	6-12	√	√		√	√	√	√	√	√	√	√	√	√	√				√	√
ART	42.5	9-12	√	√	√	√	√	√	√	√	√	√	√	√	√	√			√	√	√
DAY 43 UNIQUENESS																					
X	43.1	6-9	√	√	√	√	√	√	√	√	√	√	√	√		√					√
ART	43.2	6-12	√	√	√	√	√	√	√	√	√	√	√	√	√			√			√
ART	43.3	9-12	√	√	√	√	√	√	√	√			√	√	√	√		√		√	√
ART	43.4	9-12	√	√			√	√		√		√	√	√	√	√				√	√
DAY 44 COOPERATION																					
X	44.1	6-9	√	√		√	√	√	√	√	√	√	√	√	√	√					√
ART	44.2	9-12	√	√		√	√	√		√		√	√			√					√
X	44.3	6-8	√																		√
X	44.4	6-9	√	√		√	√	√	√	√	√	√	√	√	√						√
IS	44.5	9-10	√	√		√	√	√	√	√	√		√		√	√					√
RES	44.6	10-12	√	√		√	√	√	√	√		√	√		√	√					√
DAY 45 MASTERY																					
X	45.1	6-12	√	√		√	√		√	√			√	√		√					
LA	45.2	9-12	√	√		√	√	√	√	√		√	√	√	√	√				√	√
LA	45.3	10-12	√	√	√	√	√	√	√	√	√	√	√	√	√	√				√	√
LA	45.4	8-12	√	√	√	√	√	√	√	√	√	√	√	√	√	√	√	√	√		√
DAY 46 COMPASSION																					
ART	46.1	6-12	√	√	√	√	√	√	√	√	√	√	√	√	√	√		√			√
LA	46.1	6-8	√	√	√	√	√	√	√	√	√	√	√	√	√	√		√			√
RES	46.1	6-8	√	√		√	√	√	√	√		√	√	√	√	√				√	√
X	46.1	9-12	√	√	√	√	√	√	√	√	√	√	√	√	√	√	√			√	√
LA	46.1	10-12	√	√	√	√	√	√	√	√	√	√	√	√	√	√	√	√		√	√
LA	46.1	9-12	√	√	√	√	√	√	√	√	√	√	√	√	√	√	√			√	√

Column headers: GRADE LEVEL (GL), DEVELOPING ORAL COMM. (OD), POINT OF VIEW (R1), FACT FROM OPINION (R2), DRAWING CONCLUSIONS (R3), INTERPRET EVENTS & ABSTRACT (R4), USE CONTEXT CLUES (R5), UNDERSTAND CAUSE & EFFECT (R6), UNDERSTAND MAIN IDEA (R7), COMPARE & CONTRAST (R8), NARRATIVE (W1), DESCRIPTIVE (W2), PERSUASIVE (W3), EXPOSITORY (W4), RES. & APPLICATION (W5), LIT. RESPONSE (W6), POETRY/PROSE (W7), LETTER WRITING (W8), JOURNAL RECORD KEEPING (W9), LANGUAGE MECHANICS (W10)

ICON	No.	GL	OD	R1	R2	R3	R4	R5	R6	R7	R8	W1	W2	W3	W4	W5	W6	W7	W8	W9	W10
DAY 47	**DISARMAMENT**																				
ART	47.1	6-9	√	√	√	√	√	√	√	√	√	√	√	√	√	√	√	√			√
X	47.2	9-12	√	√	√	√	√	√	√	√	√	√	√	√	√	√	√				√
RES	47.3	6-8	√	√	√	√	√	√	√	√	√	√	√	√	√	√				√	√	√
RES	47.4	9-12	√	√	√	√	√	√	√	√	√	√	√	√	√	√					√	√
X	47.5	10-12	√	√	√	√	√	√	√	√	√	√	√	√	√	√				√	√	√
MATH	47.6	10-12	√	√	√	√	√	√	√	√	√	√	√	√	√	√						√
X	47.7	10-12	√	√	√	√	√	√	√	√	√	√	√	√	√	√						√
RES	47.8	9-12	√	√	√	√	√	√	√	√	√	√	√	√	√	√					√	√
RES	47.9	10-12	√	√	√	√	√	√	√	√	√	√	√	√	√	√					√	√
MATH	47.10	10-12	√	√	√	√	√	√	√	√	√	√	√	√	√	√					√	√
TA	47.11	9-12	√	√	√	√	√	√	√	√	√	√	√	√	√	√					√	√
DAY 48	**ECOLOGY**																				
LS	48.1	6-12	√	√	√	√	√	√	√	√	√	√	√	√	√	√						√
LS	48.2	6-8	√	√	√	√	√	√	√	√	√	√	√	√	√	√						√
RES	48.3	9-12	√	√	√	√	√	√	√	√	√	√	√	√	√	√					√	√
RES	48.4	9-12	√	√	√	√	√	√	√	√	√	√	√	√	√	√					√	√
X	48.5	6-8	√	√	√	√	√	√	√	√	√	√	√	√	√	√	√				√	√
DAY 49	**HONOR**																				
ART	49.1	6-12	√	√	√	√	√	√	√	√	√	√	√	√	√	√	√	√	√	√	√
ART	49.2	6-9	√	√	√	√	√	√	√	√	√	√	√	√	√	√	√	√	√		√
LA	49.3	6-9	√	√	√	√	√	√	√	√	√	√	√	√					√			√
LA	49.4	6-12	√	√	√	√	√	√	√	√	√	√	√			√	√		√			√
LA	49.5	6-12	√	√	√	√	√	√	√	√	√	√	√			√	√		√			√
X	49.6	8-12	√	√	√	√	√	√	√	√	√	√	√			√	√		√		√	√
DAY 50	**CHOICE**																				
RES	50.1	9-12	√	√	√	√	√	√	√	√	√	√	√	√	√	√				√	√	√
LA	50.2	6-8	√	√	√	√	√	√	√	√	√	√	√	√	√	√	√	√	√			√
TA	50.3	6-12	√	√	√	√	√	√	√	√	√	√	√	√	√	√			√		√	√
X	50.4	10-12	√	√	√	√	√	√	√	√	√	√	√	√	√	√	√				√	√
DAY 51	**ADVOCACY**																				
LA	51.1	6-12	√	√	√	√	√	√	√	√	√	√	√	√	√	√	√	√	√		√	√
X	51.2	9-12	√	√	√	√	√	√	√	√	√	√	√	√	√	√					√	√
X	51.3	6-12	√	√	√	√	√	√	√	√	√	√	√	√	√	√				√	√	√
RES	51.4	9-12	√	√	√	√	√	√	√	√	√	√	√	√	√	√				√	√	√
X	51.5	11-12	√	√	√	√	√	√	√	√	√	√	√	√	√	√				√	√	√
RES	51.6	9-12	√	√	√	√	√	√	√	√	√	√	√	√	√	√				√	√	√

ICON	No.	GL	OD	R1	R2	R3	R4	R5	R6	R7	R8	W1	W2	W3	W4	W5	W6	W7	W8	W9	W10
DAY 52 EQUALITY																					
SS	52.1	6-12	√	√	√	√	√	√	√	√	√	√	√	√	√	√	√			√	√
RES	52.2	9-12	√	√	√	√	√	√	√	√	√	√	√	√	√	√	√			√	√
LS	52.3	10-12	√	√	√	√	√	√	√	√	√	√	√	√	√	√	√			√	√
RES	52.4	10-12	√	√	√	√	√	√	√	√	√	√	√	√	√	√				√	√
RES	52.5	10-12	√	√	√	√	√	√	√	√	√	√	√	√	√	√				√	√
X	52.6	10-12	√	√	√	√	√	√	√	√	√	√	√	√	√	√				√	√
X	52.7	9-12	√	√	√	√	√	√	√	√	√	√	√	√	√	√				√	√
X	52.8	10-12	√	√	√	√	√	√	√	√	√	√	√	√	√	√	√			√	√
DAY 53 ACTION																					
LA	53.1	6-12	√	√		√	√	√	√	√		√	√	√	√	√				√	√
SS	53.2	6-9	√	√	√		√	√		√	√	√	√	√	√					√	√
LA	53.3	6-9	√	√		√	√	√	√	√		√	√	√							√
RES	53.4	6-7	√			√	√	√	√	√			√	√	√						
ART	53.5	6-9	√	√	√		√	√	√	√		√	√		√			√			√
X	53.6	9-12	√	√		√	√	√	√	√	√		√	√		√					√
RES	53.7	10-12	√	√		√	√	√	√	√	√	√	√	√	√	√					√
LA	53.8	6-12		√																	
RES	53.9	6-9		√																	
DAY 54 GIVING																					
LA	54.1	6-8	√	√	√	√	√	√	√	√	√	√	√	√	√	√	√			√	√
ART	54.2	9-12	√	√	√	√	√	√	√	√	√	√	√	√	√	√					√
SS	54.3	6-9	√	√		√	√		√			√	√	√	√						√
LA	54.4	10-12	√	√	√	√	√	√	√	√	√	√	√	√	√	√			√	√	√
X	54.5	6-12	√	√			√	√		√		√	√	√	√						√
X	54.6	6-9								√										√	
DAY 55 RESPONSIBILITY																					
X	55.1	6-9	√	√		√	√	√	√	√	√	√	√	√	√	√				√	
SS	55.2	9-12	√	√	√	√		√	√	√	√			√							√
LS	55.3	9-12	√	√		√	√	√	√	√				√						√	√
ART	55.4	6-12	√	√	√	√	√	√	√	√	√	√	√	√	√	√				√	√
X	55.5	9-12	√	√	√	√	√	√	√	√	√	√	√	√	√					√	
LA	55.6	10-12	√	√	√	√	√	√	√	√	√	√	√	√	√	√			√	√	√
TA	55.7	10-12	√	√	√	√	√	√	√	√	√	√	√	√	√	√	√	√		√	√
DAY 56 SUFFICIENCY																					
LA	56.1	9-12	√	√	√	√	√	√	√	√	√	√	√	√	√	√					√
LS	56.2	6-8	√	√		√	√	√	√	√		√	√	√	√						√
LA	56.3	11-12	√	√	√	√		√	√	√	√	√	√	√	√						√
SS	56.4	8-10	√			√	√	√	√	√	√	√	√	√	√					√	
RES	56.5	10-12	√	√	√	√	√	√	√	√	√	√	√	√	√					√	√

ICON	No.	GL	OD	R1	R2	R3	R4	R5	R6	R7	R8	W1	W2	W3	W4	W5	W6	W7	W8	W9	W10
DAY 57 SERVICE																					
LA	57.1	6-12	√	√	√	√	√	√	√	√	√	√	√	√	√	√				√	√
X	57.2	6-12	√	√	√	√	√	√	√	√	√	√	√	√	√	√				√	
X	57.3	6-12	√	√	√	√	√	√	√	√	√	√	√	√	√	√				√	
X	57.4	6-12	√	√	√	√	√	√	√	√	√	√	√	√	√	√				√	
RES	57.5	6-12	√	√	√	√	√	√	√	√	√	√	√	√	√	√		√	√	√	√
DAY 58 CITIZENSHIP																					
SS	58.1	6-12	√	√	√	√	√	√	√	√	√	√	√	√	√	√			√		√
SS	58.2	10-12	√	√	√	√	√	√	√	√	√	√	√	√	√	√					√
SS	58.3	9-12	√	√	√	√	√	√	√	√	√	√	√	√	√	√	√	√	√	√	√
LA	58.4	9-12	√	√	√	√	√	√	√	√	√	√	√	√	√	√					√
X	58.5	9-12	√	√	√	√	√	√	√	√	√	√	√	√	√	√	√		√	√	√
DAY 59 INTERVENTION																					
LA	59.1	6-8	√	√	√	√	√	√	√	√	√	√	√	√	√	√					√
X	59.2	10-12	√	√	√	√	√	√	√	√	√	√	√	√	√	√					
LA	59.3	9-12	√	√		√	√	√	√	√		√	√	√	√	√					√
ART	59.4	10-12		√	√		√	√	√	√		√	√	√	√						√
X	59.5	10-12	√	√	√	√	√	√	√	√	√	√	√	√	√	√					√
DAY 60 WITNESSING																					
LA	60.1	6-8		√		√	√	√	√		√	√	√	√						√	√
LA	60.2	9-12	√	√	√	√	√	√		√	√	√	√			√				√	√
SS	60.3	11-12	√	√	√	√	√	√	√	√	√	√	√	√	√	√				√	√
SS	60.4	11-12	√	√	√	√	√	√	√	√	√		√		√	√					√
RES	60.5	11-12	√	√	√	√	√	√	√	√	√		√		√	√	√				√
DAY 61 PEACE																					
X	61.1	6-9	√	√			√			√		√	√								√
X	61.2	6-8	√	√		√	√			√			√								√
ART	61.3	6-12	√	√		√	√	√		√			√		√						√
ART	61.4	6-8	√	√			√	√		√		√	√		√	√		√			√
LA	61.5	6-8	√	√		√	√			√			√		√			√			√
RES	61.6	9-12	√			√	√	√	√	√	√	√	√			√	√				√
ART	61.7	9-12	√	√		√	√			√		√	√		√		√			√	√
LA	61.8	6-12	√	√			√	√	√	√		√	√	√		√					√
LA	61.9									√											
DAY 62 COMMITMENT																					
X	62.1	6-12	√	√						√		√	√								
LA	62.2	9-12	√	√			√			√		√	√		√						√
LA	62.3	10-12	√	√		√	√	√		√		√	√		√	√				√	√
X	62.4	6-9	√	√		√		√	√	√		√	√	√				√			
RES	62.5	10-12	√	√	√	√	√	√	√	√			√	√	√	√					√
X	62.6	9-12	√				√			√		√	√					√	√		√

ICON	No.	GRADE LEVEL GL	DEVELOPING ORAL COMM. OD	POINT OF VIEW R1	FACT FROM OPINION R2	DRAWING CONCLUSIONS R3	INTERPRET EVENTS & ABSTRACT R4	USE CONTEXT CLUES R5	UNDERSTAND CAUSE & EFFECT R6	UNDERSTAND MAIN IDEA R7	COMPARE & CONTRAST R8	NARRATIVE W1	DESCRIPTIVE W2	PERSUASIVE W3	EXPOSITORY W4	RES. & APPLICATION W5	LIT. RESPONSE W6	POETRY/PROSE W7	LETTER WRITING W8	JOURNAL RECORD KEEPING W9	LANGUAGE MECHANICS W10
DAY 63	**RELEASE**																				
X	63.1	10-12	√	√		√	√	√	√	√		√	√	√							
LA	63.2	6-9	√	√		√	√	√	√			√	√								
ART	63.3	6-8	√	√		√	√	√	√	√		√	√								
TA	63.4	10-12	√	√	√	√	√	√	√	√	√		√		√						√
DAY 64	**CELEBRATION**																				
ART	64.1		√	√	√	√	√	√	√	√	√		√		√	√				√	
X	64.2		√	√		√	√		√			√	√						√	√	
ART	64.3		√	√	√	√	√	√	√	√	√	√	√	√	√	√	√	√	√	√	√

VOCABULARY WORKSHEET

Word —————————————————— **Part of Speech** ——————————

Definition ——————————————————————————————————

Examples ——————————————————————————————————

Synonyms ——————————————————————————————————

Sentence ——————————————————————————————————

——————————————————————————————————————

Word —————————————————— **Part of Speech** ——————————

Definition ——————————————————————————————————

Examples ——————————————————————————————————

Synonyms ——————————————————————————————————

Sentence ——————————————————————————————————

——————————————————————————————————————

Word —————————————————— **Part of Speech** ——————————

Definition ——————————————————————————————————

Examples ——————————————————————————————————

Synonyms ——————————————————————————————————

Sentence ——————————————————————————————————

——————————————————————————————————————

LITERARY RESPONSE WORKSHEET

I. Rewrite the quote as you consider its meaning:

_____

_____

_____

_____

_____

II. What do you think the author means?

_____

_____

_____

_____

III. Does it relate to events in the news or in your life?
Do you agree with the author's point of view? Why or why not?

_____

_____

_____

_____

_____

_____

GLOBAL PERSPECTIVE/DECADE OF NONVIOLENCE

As a participant in this

Season for Nonviolence,

you have become part of

an international movement

for a culture of

peace and nonviolence.

DECADE OF NONVIOLENCE

The materials included in this section are intended to provide you with a context for your participation in the *Season for Nonviolence* campaign. The *Season for Nonviolence* is aligned with the United Nations' resolution for an International Decade of Nonviolence for the Children of the World (2001–2010). We have included the following documents to assist you:

- A Culture of Peace and Nonviolence:
    The Challenge of the Next Century
    What is a Culture of Nonviolence?

- Appeal of the Nobel Peace Prize Laureates for the Children of the World

- International Decade for a Culture of Peace and Nonviolence for the Children of the World (2001–2010)

- The Nobel Peace Laureates Manifesto 2000

A growing number of schools, community groups, religious organizations, and national groups are joining us in support of the Nobel Laureates Appeal. Perhaps your class and/or your school would like to create their own resolution and forward it to us at *A Season for Nonviolence – Los Angeles, 1473 Wilshire Blvd., #472, Santa Monica, CA 90403.*

A sample is included:

- *A Season for Nonviolence – Los Angeles* Pledge for Nonviolence

- Principles of Nonviolence
    Common Peace, Center for the Advancement of Nonviolence

In addition, we have included the following historic documents that you may find useful in introducing principles of nonviolence:

- Six Principles of Nonviolence: The Kingian Philosophy, as described in *Stride Toward Freedom,* Dr. Martin Luther King, Jr., and summarized by Dr. Bernard Lafayette

- "Eight Blunders of the World" by Mahatma Gandhi and "Eight Blunders" defined by Arun Gandhi

A CULTURE OF PEACE AND NONVIOLENCE

THE CHALLENGE OF THE NEXT CENTURY

UNITED NATIONS PROCLAMATIONS ON PEACE AND NONVIOLENCE

On November 10, 1998, the United Nations General Assembly proclaimed the year 2000 to be The Year for the Culture of Peace. On the same day, the international body went on to declare the years 2001–2010 to be the International Decade for a Culture of Peace and Nonviolence for the Children of the World.

How Did We Get Here?

These much acclaimed and world challenging resolutions came as a result of a campaign initiated in 1996 by Pierre Marchand of the International Fellowship of Reconciliation affiliate, Partage, SC, along with Nobel Peace Laureates Mairead Corrigan McGuire of the International Fellowship of Reconciliation Northern Ireland affiliate, Peace People, and Adolfo Pérez Esquivel, former Latin American coordinator of Service of Peace and Justice/Servicio Paz y Justicia.

In 1997, an appeal of the Nobel Peace Laureates, signed by 23 Nobel Laureates, which included every living Peace Laureate, was sent to heads of state of all member countries of the general assembly. (Before her passing, Mother Teresa had added her name from her hospital bed.) Thousands of signatures from around the world had been gathered by IFOR and its branches and affiliates, in support of dedicating the first decade of the new millennium to building a culture of world-wide nonviolence.

Who Will Be Involved?

The proclamation passed by the UN invites each member state to teach the principles of nonviolence at every level of society. UN bodies, nongovernmental organizations (NGOs), educational institutions, religious leaders and communities, the media, performing artists, and civil societies are called upon to support the decade for the benefit of the children of the world.

Fellowship of Reconciliation. (1999).

The Challenge of the next century.

Fellowship Magazine, May-June, no page.

Reprinted with permission from Fellowship of Reconciliation

Box 271 Nyack, NY 10960-0271 • (914) 358-0271

FOR@forusa.org www.nonviolence.org.

Janet Chisholm contact for Culture of Peace and Nonviolence

Now the time has come to experiment with nonviolence in all areas of human conflict, and that means nonviolence on an international scale.
  —Dr. Martin Luther King, Jr.

WHAT IS A CULTURE OF NONVIOLENCE?

A culture of nonviolence is a culture based on the values of love, compassion, justice, and harmony. It rejects violence as a means of solving problems. Instead, it embraces communication, cooperative decision making, and nonviolent conflict resolution. It is the basis of freedom, security, and equitable relationships. It is a process for a life of reconciliation, nurturing inner peace, and personal transformation.

How Shall We Envision a Culture of Nonviolence?

A culture of nonviolence is one in which children are taught conflict resolution and respect for human rights, both at home and in school.

A culture of nonviolence encourages individual and group nonviolent action for societal and structural systems that assure racial and economic justice.

A culture of nonviolence is one in which governments take seriously the call for the abolition of nuclear weapons and carry out plans to dismantle weapons of war, leading the way toward greater international cooperation and the equitable distribution of global resources.

A culture of nonviolence fosters the nonviolent understanding present in all spiritual practices. People of faith are united in their quest for peace and justice.

A culture of nonviolence recognizes the richness of all our diverse societies. It celebrates the nonviolent traditions and histories present within each society.

We are constantly being astonished these days at the amazing discoveries in the field of violence.
But I maintain that far more undreamt of and seemingly impossible discoveries will be made in the field of nonviolence.
  —Mohandas Gandhi

Fellowship of Reconciliation. (1999).

The Challenge of the next century.

Fellowship Magazine, May-June, no page.

Reprinted with permission from Fellowship of Reconciliation

Box 271 Nyack, NY 10960-0271 • (914) 358-0271

FOR@forusa.org www.nonviolence.org.

Janet Chisholm contact for Culture of Peace and Nonviolence

For the Children of the World

To: **Heads of State of all member countries of the General Assembly of the United Nations**
From: **Nobel Peace Prize Laureates**

Today, in every single country throughout the world, there are many children silently suffering the effects and consequences of violence.

This violence takes many different forms: between children on the street, at school, in family life, and in the community. There is physical violence, psychological violence, socioeconomic violence, environmental violence, and political violence. Many children – too many children – live a "culture of violence."

We wish to contribute to reduce their suffering. We believe that each child can discover, by himself, that violence is not inevitable. We can offer hope, not only to the children of the world, but to all humanity, by beginning to create, and build, a new Culture of Nonviolence.

For this reason, we address this solemn appeal to all Heads of State of all member countries of the General Assembly of the United Nations, for the UN General Assembly to declare:

■ That the first decade of the new millenium, the years 2000–2010, be declared the "Decade for a Culture of Nonviolence;"

■ That at the start of the decade the year 2000 be declared the "Year of Education for Nonviolence;"

■ That nonviolence be taught at every level in our societies during this decade, to make the children of the world aware of the real, practical meaning and benefits of nonviolence in their daily lives, in order to reduce the violence, and consequent suffering, perpetrated against them and humanity in general.

Together we can build a new culture of nonviolence for humankind which will give hope to all humanity, and in particular, to the children of our world.

With deepest respect,
Nobel Peace Prize Laureates

1965 UNICEF	1970 Norman Borley	1977 Betty Williams	1977 Mairead Corrigan Maguire
1979 Mother Teresa	1980 Adolfo Perez Exquivel	1983 Lech Walesa	1984 Desmond Moilo Tutu
1986 Elie Wiesel	1987 Oscar Arias Sanchez	1969 Dalai Lama (Tenzin Gyalso)	1990 Mikhail Sergeyevich Gorbachov
1991 Aung San Suu Kyi	1993 Frederik Willem de Klerk	1993 Nelson Mandela	1994 Yassar Arafat
1994 Shimon Péres	1995 Joseph Rotblat	1998 José Ramos-Horta	1996 Carlos Felipe Ximenes Belo

Fellowship of Reconciliation. (1999). The Challenge of the next century. Fellowship Magazine, May-June, no page.
Reprinted with permission from Fellowship of Reconciliation
Box 271 Nyack, NY 10960-0271 • (914) 358-0271
FOR@forusa.org www.nonviolence.org.
Janet Chisholm contact for Culture of Peace and Nonviolence

International Decade for a Culture of Peace and Nonviolence for the Children of the World (2001–2010)

The General Assembly,

Aware that the task of the United Nations to save future generations from the scourge of war requires transformation towards a culture of peace, which consists of peace, which consists of values, attitudes, and behaviors that reflect and inspire social interaction and sharing based on the principles of freedom, justice and democracy, all human rights, tolerance and solidarity, that reject violence and endeavor to prevent conflicts by tackling their root causes to solve problems through dialogue and negotiation and guarantees the full exercise of all rights and the means to participate fully in the development process of their society;

Recognizing that enormous harm and suffering are caused to children through different forms of violence at every level of society throughout the world and that a culture of peace and nonviolence promotes respect for life and dignity of every human being without prejudice or discrimination of any kind;

Recognizing also the role of education in constructing a culture of peace and nonviolence, in particular teaching the practice of nonviolence to children, which will promote the purposes and principles embodied in the Charter of the United Nations;

Emphasizing that the promotion of a culture of peace and nonviolence, by which children learn to live together in peace and harmony that will contribute to the strengthening of international peace and cooperation, should emanate from the adults and be instilled in children;

Underlining that the proposed international decade for a culture of peace and nonviolence for the children of the world will contribute to the promotion of a culture of peace based on the principles embodied in the Charter and on respect for human rights, democracy, and tolerance, the promotion of development, education for peace, the free flow of information, and wider participation of women

as an integral approach to preventing violence and conflicts, and efforts aimed at the creation of conditions for peace and its consolidation;

Convinced that such a decade, at the beginning of the new millennium, would greatly assist the efforts of the international community to foster peace, harmony, all human rights, democracy and development throughout the world:

1. *Proclaims* the period 2001–2010 as the International Decade for A Culture of Peace and Nonviolence for the Children of the World.

2. *Invites* the Secretary-General to submit, in consultation with Member States, relevant United Nations bodies and non-governmental organizations, a report to the General Assembly at its fifty-fifth session and a draft program of action to promote the implementation of the Decade at local, national, regional, and international levels, and to coordinate the activities of the Decade;

3. *Invites* Member States to take the necessary steps to ensure that the practice of peace and nonviolence is taught at all levels in their respective societies, including in educational institutions;

4. *Calls upon* relevant United Nations bodies, in particular the United Nations Educational, Scientific, and Cultural Organization and the United Nations Children's Fund, and invites non-governmental organizations, religious bodies and groups, educational institutions, artists, and the media actively to support the Decade for the benefit of every child of the world;

5. *Decides* to consider, at its fifty-fifth session, the question of the International Decade for a Culture of Peace and Nonviolence for the Children of the World (2001–2010), under the agenda item entitled "Culture of Peace." ■

Fifty-fifth plenary meeting 10 November 1998

Fellowship of Reconciliation. (1999).
The Challenge of the next century. Fellowship Magazine, May-June, no page
Reprinted with permission from Fellowship of Reconciliation
Box 271 Nyack, NY 10960-0271 • (914) 358-0271
FOR@forusa.org www.nonviolence.org.
Janet Chisholm contact for Culture of Peace and Nonviolence

PEACE IS IN OUR HANDS
Manifesto 2000 for a culture of peace and non-violence

These are the six pledges of Manifesto 2000 which already bears the signatures of Noble Peace Prize Laureates.

As we continue the declaration for a decade of peace, you too can sign it.

I, who have signed the Manifesto 2000 for a culture of peace and non-violence, pledge in my daily life, family, work, community, country and region to:

RESPECT ALL LIFE — **respect the life** and dignity of every person without discrimination or prejudice.

REJECT VIOLENCE — **practice active non-violence,** rejecting violence in all its forms: physical, sexual, psychological, economical and social, in particular towards the most deprived and vulnerable such as children and adolescents;

SHARE WITH OTHERS — **share my time and material resources** in a spirit of generosity to put an end to exclusion, injustice and political and economic oppression;

LISTEN TO UNDERSTAND — **defend freedom of expression and cultural diversity** giving preference always to dialogue and listening rather than fanaticism, defamation and the rejection of others;

PRESERVE THE PLANET — **promote consumer behavior that is responsible** and development practices that respect all forms of life and preserve the balance of nature on the planet;

REDISCOVER SOLIDARITY — **contribute to the development of my community,** with the full participation of women and the respect for Democratic principles, in order to create together new forms of solidarity.

Surname: _____

First name: _____

Date of birth: Day _____ Month _____ Year_____ Sex ☐ Female ☐ Male

Address: _____

_____

Phone: _____ Email: _____

Source: www3.unesco.org/manifesto2000/default.asp. Used with permission

Season for Nonviolence Pledge

Carry the Vision

"The nonviolent approach does not immediately change the heart of the oppressor. It first does something to the hearts and souls of those committed to it. It gives them new self respect; it calls up resources of strength and courage they did not know they had."

–Dr. Martin Luther King, Jr.

"My message is my life"-Mahatma Gandhi

I, _____,
join with the A Season for Nonviolence community, in nurturing a society that honors the dignity and worth of every human being. In this way, I affiliate myself with Nobel Peace Laureates and the United Nations in declaring the first decade of the new millennium, the Decade of Nonviolence.

As I choose to live with a reverence for Life, as I stand for a just and compassionate world, I become part of what Dr. Martin Luther King, Jr. named the "beloved community," a fellowship of individuals and organizations committed to the realization of peace and equity through the active practice of nonviolence principles.

I am dedicated to moving the world in the direction of peace through my daily nonviolent choice and action.

_____
Signature/Date

Common Peace,
Center for the Advancement of Nonviolence
Principles of Nonviolence

Nonviolence means to:

❖ Honor the dignity and worth of every human being and the sacredness of all life.

❖ Practice mindful consumption. "Live simply so that others might simply live."
—Gandhi

❖ Listen deeply with an intent to understand another human being and the causes behind conflict. Address the fundamental causes of violence in order to create lasting peace.

❖ Actively challenge ignorance, prejudice, poverty, oppression, and exploitation without resorting to violence. Work for justice, healing, and reconciliation.

❖ Recognize love as the power of the human spirit to triumph over injustice, social inequity and suffering.

❖ Cultivate moral strength and courage through education, community building, and creative nonviolent action.

❖ Cultivate nonviolent ethics and/or a spiritual practice of nonviolence.

❖ Take responsibility for being a peacemaker wherever you are—in your life, family, school, work, community, nation, and world.

A10

The Six Kingian Principles of Nonviolence

Kingian Nonviolence is an outgrowth of the traditions established by Tolstoy, Thoreau, Gandhi and the three historic peace churches: the Brethren, Mennonites and Quakers. Its distinction from these earlier nonviolent approaches is that it elevated nonviolence to become a third force in society, a social movement that transformed both the structures of society and its participants. It called forth a new level of personal and social responsibility as well as moral accountability.

The philosophy of Kingian Nonviolence has its roots in the collective leadership of an era as well as in Dr. King's personal pursuit of truth through his intellectual investigations and the social movements he led. His individual philosophy was deeply rooted in the Judeo-Christian tradition, but it was informed by his examination of other nonviolent traditions.

The Six Principles of Kingian Nonviolence were initially described in a chapter in Dr. King's first book, *Stride Toward Freedom*, published in 1958. The book was both a personal reflection on his experiences in the Montgomery Movement (1954–56) and an interpretation of its meaning for society. There is no more concise and comprehensive statement about the principles of nonviolence nor is there a better introduction to the philosophy than the essay, "Pilgrimage to Nonviolence."

Principle One: Nonviolence is a way of life for courageous people. It is a positive force confronting the forces of injustice, and utilizes the righteous indignation and the spiritual, emotional, and intellectual capabilities of people as the vital force for change and reconciliation.

Principle Two: The Beloved Community is the framework for the future. The nonviolent concept is an overall effort to achieve a reconciled world by raising the level of relationships among people to a height where justice prevails and persons attain their full human potential.

Principle Three: Attack forces of evil, not persons doing evil. The nonviolent approach helps one analyze the fundamental conditions, policies and practices of the conflict rather than reacting to one's opponents or their personalities.

Principle Four: Accept suffering without retaliation for the sake of the cause to achieve the goal. Self-chosen suffering is redemptive and helps the movement grow in a spiritual as well as a humanitarian dimension. The moral authority of voluntary suffering for a goal communicates the concern to one's own friends and community as well as to the opponent.

Principle Five: Avoid internal violence of the spirit as well as external physical violence. The nonviolent attitude permeates all aspects of the campaign. It provides a mirror type reflection of the reality of the condition to one's opponent and the community at large. Specific activities must be designed to help maintain a high level of spirit and morale during a nonviolent campaign.

Principle Six: The universe is on the side of justice. Truth is universal and human society and each human being is oriented to the just sense of order of the universe. The fundamental values in all of the world's great religions include the concept that the moral arc of the universe bends towards justice. For the nonviolent practitioner, nonviolence introduces a new moral context in which nonviolence is both the means and the end.

The Six Principles of Nonviolence establish the value base of the Kingian Philosophy. This foundation enables the practitioner of nonviolence to intervene in violent or violence-prone situations as a moral action with compassion for the people involved and as an act of community. It is this moral position on issues of human rights and responsibilities that make it possible for the larger public to respond to the movement for nonviolent social change.

From Layfayette and Jehnsen (1995) The Briefing Booklet: An orientation to the Kingian nonviolence conflict reconciliation. Reprinted with permission.

GANDHI'S EIGHT BLUNDERS OF THE WORLD

Mohandas K. Gandhi was convinced much of the violence in society and in our personal lives stems from the passive violence that we commit against each other. He described these acts of passive violence as the Seven Blunders. Grandfather gave me the list in 1947 just before we left India to return to South Africa where my father, Manilal, Gandhi's second son, and my mother, Sushila, worked for nonviolent change. In the Indian tradition of adding one's knowledge to the ancient wisdom being passed on, and in keeping with what Grandfather said and wrote about *responsibility*, I have added an eighth item to the list of blunders.

THE EIGHT BLUNDERS

Wealth Without Work

Pleasure Without Conscience

Knowledge Without Character

Commerce Without Morality

Science Without Humanity

Worship Without Sacrifice

Politics Without Principles

and

Rights Without Responsibilities

What did Mohandas K. Gandhi mean?

Wealth Without Work: This includes playing the stock market, gambling, sweat-shop slavery, over-estimating one's worth (i.e., like some heads of corporations drawing exorbitant salaries which are not always commensurate with the work they do). Gandhi's idea originates from the ancient Indian practice of Tenant Farmers (Zamindari). The poor were made to slog on the farms while the rich raked in the profits. With capitalism and materialism spreading so rampantly around the world, the gray area between an honest day's work and sitting back and profiting from other people's labor is growing wider. To conserve the resources of the world and share these resources equitably with all so that everyone can aspire to a good standard of living, Gandhi believed people should take only as much as they honestly need. The United States provides a typical example. The country spends an estimated $200 billion a year on manufacturing cigarettes, alcohol and allied products which harm people's health. What the country spends in terms of providing medical and research facilities to provide and find cures for health hazards caused by over-indulgence in tobacco and alcohol is sorely lacking and mind-blowing. "There is enough for everyone's need but not for everyone's greed," Gandhi said.

Pleasure Without Conscience: This is connected to wealth without work. People find imaginative and dangerous ways of bringing excitement to their otherwise dull lives. Their search for pleasure and excitement often ends up costing society very heavily. Taking drugs and playing dangerous games causes avoidable health problems that cost the world hundreds of billions of dollars in direct and indirect health care facilities. Many of these problems are self-induced, or ailments caused by careless attitudes. The United States spends more than $250 billion on leisure activities while 25 million children die each year because of hunger, malnutrition, and lack of medical facilities.

Irresponsible and unconscionable acts of sexual pleasure and indulgence also cost the people and the country very heavily. Not only do young people lose their childhood but innocent babies are brought into the world and often left to the care of the society. The emotional, financial, and moral price is heavy on everyone.

Gandhi believed pleasure must come from within the soul and excitement from serving the needy, from caring for the family, the children, and relatives. Building sound human relationships can be an exciting and adventurous activity. Unfortunately, we ignore the spiritual pleasures of life and indulge in the physical pleasures which is "pleasure without conscience."

Knowledge Without Character: Our obsession with materialism tends to make us more concerned about acquiring knowledge so that we can get a better job and make more money. A lucrative career is preferred to an illustrious character. Our educational centers emphasize career-building and not character-building. Gandhi believed if one is not able to understand one's self, how can one understand the philosophy of life. He used to tell me the story of a young man who was an outstanding student throughout his scholastic career. He scored "A's" in every subject and strove harder and harder to maintain his grades. He became a bookworm. However, when he passed with distinction and got a lucrative job, he could not deal with people nor could he build relationships. He had no time to learn these important aspects of life. Consequently, he could not live with his wife and children nor work with his colleagues. His life ended in misery. All those years of study and excellent grades did not bring him happiness. Therefore, it is not true that a person who is successful in amassing wealth is necessarily happy; education that ignores character-building is an incomplete education.

Commerce Without Morality: As in wealth without work, we indulge in commerce without morality to make more money by any means possible. Price gouging, palming off inferior products, cheating and making false claims are a few of the obvious ways in which we indulge in commerce without morality. There are also thousands of other ways in which we do immoral or unethical business. When profit-making becomes the most important aspect of business, morals and ethics usually go overboard. We cut benefits and even salaries of employees. If possible we employ "slave" labor, like the sweat shop and migrant farm workers in New York and California where workers are thoroughly exploited. Profit supercedes the needs of people. When business is unable to deal with labor it begins to mechanize. Mechanization, it is claimed, increases efficiency, but in reality it is instituted simply to make more money. Alternate jobs may be created for a few. Others will fall by the wayside and languish. Who cares? People don't matter, profits do. In more sophisticated language what we are really saying is that those who cannot keep up with the technological changes and exigencies of the times do not deserve to live—a concept on which Hitler built the Nazi Party. If society does not care for such people, can we blame them if they become criminals?

Science Without Humanity: This is science used to discover increasingly more gruesome weapons of destruction that threaten to eventually wipe our humanity. The NRA says guns don't kill people, people kill people. What they do not say is that if people didn't have guns they wouldn't have the capacity to kill as quickly or as easily. If hunting can be considered a sport, it is the most insensitive and dehumanizing sport on earth. How can killing animals bring fun and excitement to anyone? This is pleasure without conscience. When we cease to care for any life, we cease to respect all life. No other species on earth has wrought more destruction than man. Materialism has made us possessive. The more we possess the more we need to protect and so the more ruthless we become. As punishment, we will kill if someone steals to buy bread. We feel violated, but we will not bother our heads and hearts to find out why, in times of plenty, people have to live in hunger.

In order to protect and secure our homes, our neighborhoods, our countries from attacks, we use science to discover frightening weapons of destruction. The debate over the use of the atom bomb on Hiroshima and Nagasaki is a question that falls under this category. War is sometimes inevitable only because we are such ardent nationalists that we quickly label ourselves by our country of origin, by gender, by color of our skin, by the language we speak, by the religion we practice, by the town or the state we come from and so on. The labels dehumanize us, and we become mere objects. Not too long ago even wars were fought according to rules, regulations, ethics and some semblance of morality. Then Hitler changed the rules because of his monumental hate and the rest of us followed suit. Now we can obliterate cities and inhabitants by pressing a button and not be affected by the destruction because we don't see it.

Worship Without Sacrifice: One person's faith is another person's fantasy because religion has been reduced to meaningless rituals practiced mindlessly. Temples, churches, synagogues, mosques and those entrusted with the duty of interpreting religion to lay people seek to control through fear of hell, damnation, and purgatory. In the name of God they have spawned more hate and violence than any government. True religion is based on spirituality, love, compassion, understanding, and appreciation of each other whatever our beliefs may be—Christians, Jews, Hindus, Muslims, Buddhists, Atheists, Agnostics, or whatever. Gandhi believed whatever labels we put on our faith, ultimately all of us worship Truth because Truth is God. Superficially we may be very devout believers and make a tremendous public show of our worship, but if that belief, understanding, compassion, love and appreciation is not translated into our lives, prayers will have no meaning. True worship demands sacrifice not just in terms of the number of times a day we say our prayers but in how sincere we are in translating those prayers into lifestyles.

In the 1930s many Christian and Moslem clergy flocked into India to convert the millions who were oppressed as untouchables. The Christian clergy stood on street corners loudly denouncing Hinduism and proclaiming the virtues of Christianity. Months went by without a single convert accepting the offer. Frustrated, one priest asked Grandfather: "After all the oppression and discrimination that the 'untouchables' suffer under Hinduism, why is it they do not accept our offer of a better life under Christianity?"

Grandfather replied: "When you stop telling them how good Christianity is and start living it, you will find more converts than you can cope with." These words of wisdom apply to all religions of the world. We want to shout from roof-tops the virtues of our beliefs and not translate them into our lives.

Politics Without Principles: Gandhi said those who firmly believe in nonviolence should never stand for elections, but they should elect representatives who are willing to understand and practice the philosophy. Gandhi said an elected representative is one on whom you have bestowed your power of attorney. Such a person should be allowed to wield authority only as long as he or she enjoys your confidence.

When politicians indulge in power games, they act without principles. To remain in power at all cost is unethical. Gandhi said when politicians (or anyone else, for that matter) give up the pursuit of Truth they, or in the case of parties, would be doomed. Partisan politics, lobbying, bribing, and other forms of malpractice that are so rampant in politics today are also unprincipled. Politics has earned the reputation of being dirty. It is so because we made it dirty. We create power groups to lobby for our cause and are willing to do anything to achieve our goal. Not many among human kind have learned how to resist temptation, so who is to blame for the mess we find ourselves in?

Rights Without Responsibilities: We are generally willing to do anything to safeguard our rights but not much to shoulder our responsibilities towards creating a peaceful, harmonious, and understanding society. We believe that our only responsibility in a democracy is to cast our vote every four or five years. For a democracy to be healthy and honest, we need to do much more. Should we allow someone to abuse rights under a constitution so that we can preserve our own rights? Under the Freedom of Speech can we allow people to incite violence and perhaps revolution through hate, prejudice, and other forms of bigotry? Under the Right to Bear Arms can we allow people to walk about with weapons and use them freely to protect themselves and their possessions when it means killing others? If an individual can become judge, jury, and executioner, can there be a viable Rule of Law? It might be argued that violence is a form of expression of discontent. If a householder can shoot someone for trespassing with the intent to steal, why should a hungry or homeless person not have the right to kill those he suspects of having stolen his or her opportunities for livelihood? When we possess more than we deserve, we are stealing from those who do not have the opportunity to compete with our talents. Readers of *Parade* magazine were recently asked if parents or school teachers should teach children about right and wrong. Shockingly, the overwhelming response was NO. We must not impose our rights and wrongs on other people, even our own children, they argued. Isn't our entire sense of law and community and society grounded in basic concepts of right and wrong, i.e., don't harm others? Why do we try and condemn murderers and thieves? Doesn't that impose our sense of right and wrong on them, even when they believe their behavior was justified, if not right? Can we build a healthy and viable democracy on double standards?

THE FOUR CORE CONCEPTS
For Building a Culture
of Nonviolence and Peace

CULTURE

VIOLENCE

POWER

NONVIOLENCE

64 Ways to Practice Nonviolence
– Introductory Lesson

CORE CONCEPTS INTRODUCTION

The four core concepts introduced in this section provide a foundation for understanding the principles at the center of non-violence education. These core concepts provide a context for understanding the 64 ways, not as isolated lessons, but as a body of knowledge and skills for building blocks for creating peaceful people, relationships and communities.

Violence is not only a physical or verbal eruption between individuals; violence is also imbedded in the values, traditions, communication, and power structures found within the larger culture.

Culture often permits or promotes violence which is not only overtly physical but that can be economic and political as well. Culture impacts the individual's thinking and behavior as well as the way others respond to that individual's violent behavior.

Power is usually defined as "power over." Nonviolence education explores the idea of "power with." Ideas about power (What is it? How do we use it? How do we have more or less of it?) profoundly shape our individual and collective choices and behavior. They also shape the way people within communities relate to one another.

Nonviolence is the idea of power found in the heart of every human being, independent of any external circumstance or conditions. Nonviolence can transform conflict and foster peace with love, respect, compassion and education. Using this power to make the world better, to create "win-win" outcomes, to build self-mastery and affirm all life is the focus of this curriculum.

INTRODUCTORY LESSON

CULTURE

Culture consists of the beliefs and values of a people and how they express those beliefs and values through their behavior, arts, industry and institutions.

QUOTES

Culture is everything. Culture is the way we dress, the way we carry our heads, the way we walk, the way we tie our ties—it is not only the fact of writing books or building houses.

—Aime Cesaire

Writer, co-founder of Negritude movement in the 30s

No culture can live, if it attempts to be exclusive.

—Mahatma Gandhi

Codified nonviolence as a political, spiritual, and social paradigm in the 20th century

If the Aborigine drafted an I.Q. test, all of Western civilization would presumably flunk it.

—Stanley Garn

Anthropologist

QUESTIONS AND DEFINITIONS

1. **There are common elements found in every culture. Their content varies, but the structures are consistent. What are some of the universal elements of culture?**
   - ▶ Values. Examples:
     - • What is "good," what is "bad?"
     - • What are standards of beauty?
     - • What is success?
   - ▶ Social organizations/institutions
   - ▶ Rules or traditions governing behavior
   - ▶ Communication style
   - ▶ Language
   - ▶ Ceremony/ritual

2. **What are some of the institutions of culture?**
   - ▶ Family
   - ▶ Education
   - ▶ Arts and media
   - ▶ Religion (the sacred)
   - ▶ Business and economics
   - ▶ Law enforcement/military service
   - ▶ Health and human services
   - ▶ Sustainability (environmental sensitivity)
   - ▶ Recreation

3. **What are some of the subcultures that exist within the larger culture of your community?**
   Examples:
   - ▶ Ethnicity
   - ▶ Socioeconomic class
   - ▶ Religion
   - ▶ Professional affiliation

continued ▶

C U L T U R E / QUESTIONS, *continued*

- ▶ Region or neighborhood in which you live
- ▶ Arts
- ▶ Age
- ▶ Gender

- ▶ Musicians
- ▶ Athletes
- ▶ Popular kids
- ▶ Smart kids

4. **What are some of the subcultures within your school?**

ACTIVITIES

 C1.1 Draw a picture of your family. Describe your family's culture. Your description should include but not be limited to ethnicity, citizenship, religion, neighborhood, eating habits, traditions, family rules and values (i.e., who handles the money, who makes decisions, etc.).

 C1.2 Generate a class discussion about family roots and how families can help orient children to promote peace or nonviolence in their lives. Allow students to reflect on what they have learned and experienced within their family structure. Draw pictures of family or family trees, and frame the pictures with words and symbols that represent your cultural grounding with relationship to nonviolence.

 C1.3 Draw a picture of the neighborhood in which you live. What might distinguish it from other neighborhoods? Designate the things you are most proud of or the things you would like to see changed. Use small arrows and brief notes to incorporate these things into the picture.

 C1.4 Use thumbnail sketches to compare and contrast how three different cultures of your choice express the following: communication style, values, beauty and rules of behavior.

 C1.5 Write an essay, rap or poem about the cultures in which you live. Include your family, your school and your teams, clubs and neighborhood. What is unique about them? How have they contributed to who you are? What, if anything, would you like to see change?

 C1.6 Have the class develop a questionnaire for the purpose of interviewing members of one of their own cultural groups or another cultural group with which they are less familiar. After taking the interview, partner with another student and use the information obtained to identify, compare and contrast the elements of your two differing cultural groups. How did your findings coincide or differ from the perceptions you held before the interviews?

continued ▶

CULTURE / ACTIVITIES, *continued*

 C1.7 Write a brief thought paper about how your family, neighborhood or school culture helped to shape your relationship to violence or nonviolence. (To make this exercise meet classroom language objectives, ask students to use at least five common and three proper adjectives in their paper. Identify each by underlining and writing the word "common" or "proper" over the adjective.)

 C1.8 On page A15 you will find Gandhi's *Eight Blunders*. They are a brief commentary on the dangers of a culture out of balance. After reviewing the "blunders" have students select one and write a thought paper on its meaning, offering examples from their own experience. OPTIONAL: Add news headlines, photographs, or articles that illustrate your point of view.

 C1.9 On page A15 you will find Gandhi's *Eight Blunders*. They are a brief commentary on the dangers of a culture out of balance. After reviewing the "blunders" have students select one and create a skit to dramatize its meaning.

 C1.10 Return to any of the above writing exercises. How does the language you used to describe your culture or the culture of another group indicate *your* values, rules and judgments? How might someone with different values, rules, or points of view describe the very same elements of culture? How do you see different cultural points of view influence media coverage or public debate? Select several controversial issues and compare and contrast language and framing of how issues are presented.

INTRODUCTORY LESSON

VIOLENCE

"If we are honest, we find the temptation to vengeance in our own hearts. Yet we know that the first real victim of violence is the perpetrator. What Gandhi said is true: An eye for an eye results only in two blind persons."
—*Mary Evelyn Jege*

QUOTES

Violence is immoral because it thrives on hatred rather than love. Violence is impractical because it is a destruction for all. It is immoral because it seeks to humiliate the opponent rather than win his understanding; it seeks to annihilate rather than convert. Violence ends up defeating itself. It creates bitterness in the survivors and brutality in the destroyers.

—Dr. Martin Luther King, Jr.

Nonviolent U.S. Civil Rights Leader (1929-1968)

…[T]hrough violence you may murder a murderer but you can't murder murder. Through violence you may murder a liar but you can't establish truth. Through violence you can murder a hater, but you can't murder hate. Darkness cannot put out darkness. Only light can do that…

—Dr. Martin Luther King, Jr.

Author of *Where Do We Go from Here*

Violence is born from a wounded spirit… The anger that results from injured self-respect, from humiliation, erupts as violence. The culture of violence that delights in crushing and subduing others by force spreads throughout society, often amplified by the media.

—Daisaku Ikeda

Buddhist Peace Activist, Head of Sokka Gakkai International

QUESTIONS AND DEFINITIONS

1. **What is violence?**
   ▶ Anything that diminishes the dignity and worth of a human being
   ▶ A physical, mental or emotional expression
   ▶ Actions that can be perpetrated by individuals, groups and institutions
   ▶ That which stems from ignorance and suffering

2. **Identify and discuss the types of violence toward the self.**
   ▶ Mental: negative self-talk, self-judgment
   ▶ Physical: drugs and alcohol, eating disorders, self-mutilation
   ▶ Emotional: guilt, toxic shame, resentment, jealousy

continued ▶

VIOLENCE / QUESTIONS *continued*

3. **What kinds of violence do individuals perpetrate against one another? Identify and discuss inter-personal violence.**
   - ▶ Physical violence: child and domestic abuse, assault, rape, corporal punishment
   - ▶ Verbal violence: name calling, gossip, stereotyping, harassment, threats, intimidation
   - ▶ Emotional/psychic violence: control and domination, manipulation, stalking

Can words be violent?

4. **What is institutional systemic violence? Define, identify and discuss.**
   - ▶ When a culture sanctions and promotes violence toward some of its members through its institutions as overt action or lack of protection
   - ▶ The cause behind much of individual and group violence; creates an environment that promotes and sanctions this microcosmic violence
     Examples:
     - inequitable allocation of resources (unequal access to quality education, unequal access to quality health care)
     - discrimination, Jim Crow, apartheid, caste systems
     - genocide and ethnic cleansing
     - laws that provide or deny rights and opportunities to a particular group
     - inequitable enforcement of laws based on prejudice (racial profiling)
     - "redlining" re: bank loans
     - geographic political districts or zones based on race or economics
     - corporate "glass ceiling"

   - denigrating media images of groups of people (stereotyping)

5. **How has violence affected someone you know? Was it personal, inter-personal or institutional violence?**

6. **What do you believe are the root causes of violence?**
   - ▶ Toward oneself?
   - ▶ Between groups of people?
   - ▶ Between nations?
   - ▶ What facts will support your theory?
   - ▶ What is your prescription for ending violence?

7. **If you ruled the world, what is one form of violence you would eliminate? Why? How would you eliminate it without resorting to violence?**

8. **Have you ever acted in a violent manner? What made you feel violent? What did you do? Were you happy with the outcome? What were the consequences of your act inside of you? How did your behavior reflect ignorance and suffering?**

ACTIVITIES

 **C2.1** Divide the class into teams for personal, inter-personal and institutional violence. Using Post-it® notes, give everyone a few minutes to brainstorm examples of each specific category. Each group shares their examples and posts them. The large group can add and/or move examples to a more appropriate category. Debrief thoughts and feelings regarding this "culture of violence."

continued ▶

VIOLENCE / ACTIVITIES, *continued*

 C2.2 Write a short thought paper to compare and contrast what you have learned about personal, inter-personal and institutional violence. Include specific examples of each form of violence in your paper. What do you see as the relationship between these forms of violence?

 C2.3 Write a third person true story about a personal experience of violence in which you were either the victim or perpetrator. Include what happened, how those involved were affected, and how they might feel about their actions in retrospect. At the end of the story, write a second possible outcome. How could the violence have been avoided and how could the situation have been resolved nonviolently?

 C2.4 Keep a journal for three days, recording "words as violence." What did you hear? Who said it? Pay attention to how you felt when you heard it. As you review this list, what did you perceive as the effects of these violent words? What did you learn about yourself? What would you like to tell people about the power of language?

 C2.5 Draw a picture depicting what might happen when we use violent means to address violent acts in order to achieve peace. How do these pictures reflect ignorance and suffering? Discuss examples before you begin drawing. Then hang the pictures in the classroom and view them in pairs. Discuss the predominant colors and images. Come back to the larger group and report your findings. What did you learn?

 C2.6 Research the effects of types of violence in your city, state or country of birth. You can choose from war, hate crimes, bullying, teen suicide, gun violence, the death penalty, domestic violence, drug and alcohol abuse or hunger and homelessness. Be specific in your findings and include statistics. Investigate the causes, solutions, and costs, including financial, cost in lives, costs to society, etc.

C2.7 Select a current event in the news and report on the facts and the possible solutions and outcomes. If violence has already resulted, what other options may have been available? If not, how can it be averted? Advocate your solution to the class in an oral presentation.

 C2.8 Use the newspaper or the Internet to research and develop a presentation about any one specific example of institutional violence. Identify the people who are the victims of this institutional violence. What are the long term effects?

INTRODUCTORY LESSON

POWER

"Gandhi believed, and his life demonstrated, that under certain conditions all men and women have a tremendous power available to them, and their 'action becomes all-pervasive in its effects.' They become 'irresistible,' not overcoming opposition with force but melting it away, finally with its own consent."
—*Eknath Easwaran*

QUOTES

Power at its best is love implementing the demands of justice; and justice at its best is power correcting everything that stands against love.

—Dr. Martin Luther King, Jr.

Youngest person to receive the Nobel Peace Prize

Most powerful is he who has himself in his own power.

—Seneca

Advisor to Roman Emperor Nero

Nearly all men can stand adversity, but if you want to test a man's character, give him power.

—Abraham Lincoln

11th U.S. President (1809-1865)

QUESTIONS AND DEFINITIONS

1. **What is power?**
   - ▶ To influence and affect outcome; to demonstrate authority to influence and affect outcome
   - ▶ Material power or external power based on status, beauty, money, access and weapons; arises from external forces
   - ▶ Arises from internal sources; Gandhi called it "Satyagraha" or "soul force"

2. **There is power from "without" and power from "within." Describe these two kinds of power. How are they different? How are they alike?**
   - ▶ Inner power based on "Truth," (human dignity, justice and compassion)

3. **Who has the power in your family, school,** community, country? How do you know they have the power? Is this the result of internal or external power?

4. **Discuss the idea of the "power to destroy life" versus "the power to affirm life." Give examples of each. How have people and events wielding these types of power affected your life, society and history?**

5. **Power is neither good nor bad. Like electricity, it's how you choose to use it that makes it good or bad. How can power be used to help or hurt? What are examples of using your power to be an adversary or an ally?**

POWER / ACTIVITIES

ACTIVITIES

C3.1 Brainstorm as a class. Make two lists to show who has the power in various relationships and situations. Notice that you can find yourself on either list depending on the situation and social group in which you are measuring your rank.

a. older sibling	younger sibling
b. male	female
c. native born citizen	immigrant
d. immigrant	illegal immigrant
e. Anglo American	other race
f. English speaking	English as a second language
g. heterosexual	homosexual, bisexual, other
h. called "fat"	"normal" weight
i. children	adults
j. perfect health	visible or hidden disability
k. Christian	other religion
l. owns a computer	no computer

Select one of these power relationships and give examples of the privileges (the power) that group enjoys. Select one of these relationships and give examples of the privileges (the power) enjoyed by the social group that has greater rank in society. Identify ways in which the power of the social group with lesser rank is limited by laws, customs and culture.

(Based on exercise found in *Helping Teens Stop Violence*, by Allan Creighton and Paul Kivel; see Bibliography.)

C3.2 Choose a power relationship from the list above and create a poster with a caption that depicts a nonviolent message or resolution.

C3.3 Describe someone you know who is powerful from "within," not because of what they have, but because of who they are. How has that person affected your life? Can you describe a specific situation in which that person affected your outcome in a positive way?

C3.4 Write a paper about what you have learned about power and who has it—from television, music, your peers, the government or the culture with which you most strongly identify. Focus on the one area that you think has influenced and impacted you the most up until this time in your life.

C3.5 Identify three relationships in which you seem to have more power than another person. What is that experience like for you? How do you use your power, and for what purpose? How does your use of power affect the lives of others who seem to have less power? What do you imagine that experience is like for the other side? What do you see as the consequences of unequal power? Now

continued ▶

P O W E R / ACTIVITIES, *continued*

identify three relationships in which you have less power than another person. Describe the experience. Write a thought paper and include at least three insights that you have gained about yourself and power.

 C3.6 Invite a master of Tai Chi or Aikido to demonstrate the power of non-resistance, the power of an individual who finds his or her strength from within. Can people be harmless and still defend themselves? How? Facilitate a conversation defining "power" versus "force."

 C3.7 Invite a gang truce leader or a youth community peacemaker to share his or her experience of the power of peacemaking. What power did they use to get out of the cycle of violence and still take care of themselves? Have a panel of students respond to the speaker's story.

 C3.8 What did Gandhi, King, Chavez, Rosa Parks, Sister Chan Khong and other great men and women of peace accomplish? How did they affect the world? What was powerful about them? Choose one of the above and tell his or her story in the first person.

 C3.9 What is the Nobel Peace Prize? Who are some of the people who have been awarded the Nobel Peace Prize? What did they do? How were they powerful, and what gave them power? What might have happened in their communities if they had not made a commitment to nonviolence?

 C3.10 Paulo Friere said, "Washing one's hands of the conflict between the powerful and the powerless means to side with the powerful, not to be neutral." Research the work of Paulo Friere. Then write a short thought paper on what you think he meant, based on his work. Do you agree with the statement? What does this statement have to do with democracy?

INTRODUCTORY LESSON

NONVIOLENCE

"The main elements of a culture of peace will include respect for life and human rights; rejection of violence; inculcation of the principles of freedom, justice, and democracy; tolerance and solidarity among peoples; addressing root causes of conflicts; problem solving through dialogue and negotiation; freedom of expression; and full participation in development processes."
—*John Dear*

QUOTES

The nonviolent approach doesn't immediately change the heart of the oppressor. It first does something to the hearts and souls of those committed to it. It gives them new self-respect; it calls up resources of strength and courage that they didn't know they had. Finally, it reaches their opponent and so stirs his conscience that reconciliation becomes a reality.

—Dr. Martin Luther King, Jr.
Followed in the footsteps of Mahatma Gandhi to end racial segregation in the American South

A world without violence is possible if we stop trying to remake the world and start remaking ourselves.

—Arun Gandhi
Author, grandson of Mahatma Gandhi

Nonviolence is the weapon of the strong. It does not mean meek submission to the will of the evil doer, but putting one's whole soul against the will of the tyrant working under this law of our being, it is possible for a single individual to defy the whole might of an unjust empire.

—Mohandas Gandhi
Author of *My Experiments with Truth*, two and a half million people attended his funeral procession

The salvation of this human world lies nowhere else than in the human heart, in the human power to reflect, in human meekness and human responsibility.

—Vaclav Havel
Advocate of democracy
Re-elected to Czechoslovakian Presidency after resigning office

QUESTIONS AND DEFINITIONS

1. **What do you think nonviolence means? Where did you learn that meaning? Which beliefs are myths? Truths?**

2. **What is nonviolence? Explore the following definitions:**

► is based on a reverence for life

► is a way of life that honors the dignity and worth of every human being

► is a strategy for change: active resistance and commitment to justice without violence; a way of resolving violent, potentially violent and

continued ►

NONVIOLENCE / QUESTIONS, *continued*

unjust situations without resorting to violence; an intention to facilitate healing and reconciliation; opposes injustice, not the individual who commits the injustice.

▶ is foundation for culture and institutional transformation

3. Review and brainstorm anything you would add to *Common Peace, Center for the Advancement of Nonviolence* Principles of Nonviolence on page A10.

4. Discuss *The Six Kingian Principles of Nonviolence* on page A11. What do you think motivated the writing of each principle?

5. Study *Gandhi's Eight Blunders of the World* on pages A13 through A16. Find examples for each one.

6. Which principles do you find to be consistent in each of the above documents?

▶ recognizes the power of the human spirit to overcome any obstacle or condition

▶ is sourced from within; not dependent upon any outside source

▶ does not resort to violence to address violence

▶ seeks to facilitate healing and reconciliation

▶ opposes the deed and not the doer; seeks to understand and persuade

7. **What makes nonviolence power filled? Describe how it is powerful.**

▶ is not dependent on anything external; demonstrates that you can be free anywhere (discuss the life of Nelson Mandela)

▶ gives dominion over yourself, which no one can take away

▶ builds character, generates courage and fearlessness, confidence and authority

▶ is in harmony with the universe and promotes the order that confirms life

▶ breaks the cycle of violence and revenge

▶ appeals to the conscience within people; it is healing

▶ affirms and honors life and therefore has a contagious multiplying effect

▶ builds community by empowering community

▶ can heal people on both sides of an issue by fostering respect, understanding, compassion and forgiveness

▶ conquers fear through discovery of self mastery and love

8. **Discuss examples of nonviolent power in the following arenas. Can you think of others?**

▶ media/music/art
▶ political change
▶ human rights and social change
▶ labor
▶ environment
▶ your community

9. **Compare and contrast nonviolent versus violent approaches to problem solving, and outcomes they create.**

ACTIVITIES

 C4.1 Write a story about an individual who practices nonviolence (real or imaginary). What qualities does he or she possess? How do you know that he or she is a nonviolence practitioner?

continued ▶

NONVIOLENCE / ACTIVITIES, *continued*

 C4.2 Based on the elements of culture you have already discussed, describe a culture of nonviolence in words, illustrations and collage art.

 C4.3 Make a list of changes needed in order to practice nonviolence in your classroom. Create a document of commitment and have each student who wishes to participate in the practice of nonviolence sign the document. Display it in the classroom.

 C4.4 After reviewing Gandhi's Blunders, divide the class into teams to develop nonverbal role-plays about them. Let the skits stimulate discussion about values of nonviolence as expressed by Gandhi. Compare and contrast these "blunders" within the context of our current culture.

 C4.5 Write about one experience in which you resolved a conflict without resorting to violence. What did you do? What qualities and skills did it require of you? What were the long term effects of this approach?

 C4.6 Have a classroom discussion on consumption. Offer the class some statistics on drug addiction, average TV use, reduction of the rainforest, trash-site landfills or nuclear waste dumps. Have each student co-write a poem entitled "The things that we consume." Let students choose their own partners. Instruct them to have a lot of fun with this exercise. Encourage them to free associate as they write about mental and physical consumption, media consumption, food consumption, drug consumption, natural resource consumption. Students can focus on one example or many examples as they can think of. What we consume can contribute to violence or it can contribute to nonviolence.

 C4.7 Watch a video which describes the successful practice of nonviolence. Identify the values, principles and strategies of nonviolence as expressed in the film. Can you identify with the ways in which the heroes of nonviolence believe and act?

(Suggested videos: *A Force More Powerful, Gandhi, Freedom Song, Boycott, Long Night's Journey Into Day,* Bill Moyers, *Interview with Desmond Tutu on the South African Truth and Reconciliation Commission.* See Video Resources on pages 179 through 181.)

 C4.8 Gandhi's Eight Blunders are a brief commentary on the dangers of a culture out of balance. After reviewing the "blunders" in class, find an example of someone or some institution in society that is demonstrating balance through one of the following moral qualities featured in the "blunders": "Wealth from Work," "Commerce with Conscience," "Rights with Responsibilities," "Science with Humanity," or "Knowledge with Character." Write a letter to acknowledge, describe and commend the individual or institution you select on their accomplishments.

PERSONAL

INTERPERSONAL

COMMUNITY

PERSONAL

Nonviolence begins by learning how
to be less violent and more compassionate with
ourselves. We learn by building the courage to
speak and act with respect, honor and
reverence for our own being.

DAY 1

COURAGE

Eleanor Roosevelt has urged, "You must do the things that you think you cannot do." Practicing these *64 Ways* will challenge you to do things that you think you cannot do. Today, light a candle and accept the courage to practice *64 Ways* of living nonviolently.

QUOTES

Taking fear away from people and replacing it with courage is the essence of nonviolence.

—Mubarak Awad
Nonviolent Palestinian Leader

The word "courage" is derived from the French word for heart, coeur, and etymologically it means "the ability to stand by one's heart or to stand by one's core." Whenever we exhibit courage, we demonstrate the healing power of paying attention to what has heart and meaning for us. Strong-heartedness is where we have the courage to be all of who we are in our life.

—Angeles Arrien
Teacher, Author, Visionary

Every action for peace requires someone to exhibit the courage to challenge violence and inspire love.

—Thich Nhat Hanh
Buddhist Teacher, Writer, Activist, Buddhist Monk

Courage means standing with your values, principles, convictions and ideals under all circumstances—no matter what.

—Oscar Arias Sanchez
President of Costa Rica, 1986 – 1990, and 2006 to the present;
1987 Nobel Peace Laureate

Nonviolence and cowardice go ill together. I can imagine a fully armed man as a coward. Possession of arms implies an element of fear, if not cowardice. But true nonviolence is an impossibility without the possession of unadulterated fearlessness.

—Mohandas K. Gandhi
Nonviolent Leader of Civil Rights Movement in India (1869-1948)

COURAGE / QUESTIONS

QUESTIONS AND DEFINITIONS

1. What is courage? Are there different kinds of courage?

2. Can you remember a time when it took courage to try something you had never done before?

3. What is the last act of courage that you witnessed?

4. Who are some people in your life, community, ethnic or cultural group, the world or in history, who you think are courageous? What do you have in common with them?

5. Discuss the kind of courage necessary to take up arms and the kind of courage necessary to lay down arms. Discuss the kind of courage it takes to challenge violence and injustice without resorting to violence and injustice.

ACTIVITIES

 1.1 Think of something you did that took courage and write a short paragraph about what it meant to you and why.

 1.2 Write three things from your own life that you think you cannot do. Now write about someone you know who can do them. Talk about the qualities that make it possible for that other person. Then make a game plan about how you will do what you previously considered impossible for you.

 1.3 The first principle of Kingian nonviolence is, "Nonviolence is a way of life for courageous people." Write an essay on the ways in which you think it takes courage to practice nonviolence. Use appropriate tense, grammar, punctuation and spelling. If you would like to adopt a policy of nonviolence in your life, include some steps that you will take.

 1.4 Interview someone who you think demonstrates courage. As a class, determine the questions you would like this person to answer. Interviews can be written, audio taped or videotaped. Discuss what these people have in common. What can be learned from them?

 1.5 Learn about Ruby Bridges, Ari Aryaratne, Cesar Chavez, Ann Bigelow, Dolores Huerta or Jose Ramos Horta. After you research his or her life and work, write a speech that you think he or she might have given. Dress in character and present the speech to the class.

continued ▶

COURAGE / ACTIVITIES, *continued*

1.6 Create tight circles of six (6) or eight (8) students, shoulder to shoulder with hands held chest high, palms open, facing the center of the circle. Have one student stand in the center with arms folded across the chest, eyes closed. Center student says, "Falling." Circle answers, "Fall on," and the center student begins to fall gently (keeping body straight) until the circle catches the falling student and returns him to standing.

This activity should be reserved for mature groups who have established a foundation of trust. There must be an agreement that no one gets hurt. Person falling is instructed to call out, "Falling," and wait for a response from the circle. The circle responds, "Fall on" and only then does the center person fall. Facilitator should always be "spotting" and maintaining focus as the exercise continues.

Rules of the game: 1) No one gets hurt
2) Always call out before falling
3) Always establish silence and focus before falling and catching

Debrief in terms of how easy or difficult it was to trust the circle. What do trust and courage have to do with each other? Where does the "courage to fall" come from?

DAY 2

SMILING

Buddhist teacher Thich Nhat Hanh said, "If in our daily life, we can smile… not only we, but everyone will profit from it. This is the most basic kind of peace work." Today, share a smile with at least three people, knowing that your smile contributes to peace.

QUOTES

If we cannot smile, we cannot help other people to smile. If we are not peaceful, then we cannot contribute to the peace movement.

—Thich Nhat Hanh,
Zen Master, Poet

I smile to the world and the world smiles to me.
—Sister Chan Khong
Known as Sister True Emptiness, Vietnamese Buddhist activist (1938–)

QUESTIONS AND DEFINITIONS

1. What makes you smile? How can a simple smile change the way you feel?

2. What do you notice when you see someone smile at you?

3. What keeps you from smiling at others?

4. What does smiling have to do with nonviolence?

5. How do you carry the vision of nonviolence with a smile?

ACTIVITIES

2.1 Have students smile as often as they can remember to smile in a 24 hour period. Instruct them to gather information to compare and contrast their experience. Students can work in groups to chart their findings in order to draw conclusions that they can share with the class.

2.2 Identify a person at whom you would not normally smile (e.g., homeless person, policeman or someone from a different team or neighborhood). What gets in the way of a simple smile? What might happen, either good or bad? Experiment several times, then write or draw about your experience.

continued ▶

SMILING / ACTIVITIES, *continued*

 2.3.1 Tai Chi Smiling Guided Imagery—Everyone should become comfortable, close their eyes, and begin to relax their body. Talk students through relaxing their bodies from toes to brain, then tell them to put a gentle dolphin smile on their lips. Ask that they send the smile inward like a golden glow lighting up the inside of their mouth. Send the smile up to their forehead, warming and relaxing their thoughts and the inside of their skull, and continue to send the smile throughout their entire body. Students should then describe how this guided relaxation is affecting their mood when they come back to the group.

2.3.2 The next time you find yourself experiencing an upset, practice this exercise and record your experience to share with the class at a later time. Did it affect your mood, your choices, your behavior? *(Spinning Inward: Using Guided Imagery with Children for Learning, Creativity and Relaxation, by Maureen Murdock. See Student Bibliography, page 177.)*

 2.4 Experiment with frowning, scowling, smiling, etc. What do you notice about the way you feel and what you project? Compare and contrast the energy levels in your body after extended periods of time. Do this in dyads or small groups and then review your findings with the larger group.

DAY 3

GRATITUDE

On her TV show, Oprah Winfrey frequently promotes the daily practice of gratitude. Begin the day by listing five things for which you are grateful and end the day by sharing with at least one person all of the good things in your awareness that happened during that day.

QUOTES

As we express our gratitude, we must never forget that the highest appreciation is not to utter words, but to live by them.

—John Fitzgerald Kennedy
35th U.S. President (1925–1968)

Gratitude is not only the greatest of virtues, but the parent of all the others.

—Cicero
Philosopher, Politician of the Roman Republic (106–43 B.C.)

Don't pray when it rains if you don't pray when the sun shines.

—*New York Post*
October 4, 1959 issue

Gratitude is the heart's memory.

—French Proverb

Feeling grateful or appreciative of someone or something in your life actually attracts more of the things that you appreciate and value into your life.

—Christiane Northrup
Physician, Author, Visionary

QUESTIONS AND DEFINITIONS

1. What are you most grateful for in your life? For which of your own personal qualities are you grateful?

2. How do you demonstrate that gratitude? Or do you?

3. When was the last time you were moved to show your gratitude to someone else? Did you, and how?

4. What would you like to thank yourself for? How will you do it?

5. For what would you like to personally thank someone else? If you have not yet said "thank you" to that person, ask yourself why. Is it sometimes difficult to show your gratitude to others? In what way is it difficult? Easy?

continued ▶

GRATITUDE / ACTIVITIES

ACTIVITIES

 3.1 Create a personal timeline with pictures and short stories about the major things in your life for which you have been grateful (e.g., baby brother, first bicycle, etc.).

 3.2 Write about the top three things for which you are grateful in your life today and write about one way in which you could pass on that good fortune.

 3.3 Make a gratitude journal and include pictures and poems about all the things for which you are grateful in the world even if you don't actually own them (e.g., you could be grateful for airplanes even if you have never been on one).

 3.4 Write a thank you letter to someone who deserves thanks.

DAY 4

CARING

According to author Peter McWilliams, "Nonviolence toward the self is caring for oneself. Self love is a crowning sense of self-worth. It is what the Greeks call 'reverence for the self.' Real caring is not just what we say, but what we do." Make a list of at least five ways that you can take better care of yourself. Practice at least one way today.

QUOTES

We all have enough strength to bear other people's woes.

—François La Rochefoucauld
17th Century Author (1630–1680)

The activist is not the man who says the river is dirty. The activist is the man who cleans up the river.

—Ross Perot
Presidential Candidate, Reform Party; opposed the Gulf War

QUESTIONS AND DEFINITIONS

1. How can you tell that someone cares for you? How do you show others that you care? In what ways do you care for yourself?

2. How is caring for yourself and others an important ingredient of one's personal practice of nonviolence?

3. How does your family, school and community demonstrate that it cares for others (e.g., special awards, PTA, celebrations)?

4. How do you care for the community in which you live? The country? The planet?

ACTIVITIES

 4.1 Write about three areas in which you could take better care of yourself, and make a commitment to take care of yourself better in those three areas. What has not caring for yourself in certain areas cost you? What support do you need to make a change? Set goals. Create a tracking sheet. Choose a partner, coach each other and track your progress for a week.

 4.2 Have a campus care field trip. Walk around your classroom, inside and out, pick up trash and generally beautify the area. Are there larger beautification projects your class could take on, such as a garden or mural?

continued ▶

CARING / ACTIVITIES, *continued*

4.3 Make a standing circle and have everyone face clockwise. Then take one side step into the center so that each person can comfortably reach the person in front of them. Establish a tone of attention and focus before beginning. Have students put their hands on the shoulders of the person in front of them in a way that shows they care. A little neck and shoulder massage is good for mature groups. Then switch directions and do it again. Debrief in terms of how it felt to "care" for the two individuals that you contacted, in this small way. Does it matter how well you know the person? What is the relationship between caring in thought and actually taking action in another's behalf?

4.4 Consider the adoption of a class pet. Let students plan together on how they will share the feedings and other responsibilities of the pet. Can you give the pet a good home at school? What kind of pet is suitable for a classroom? Is there someone in class who wants (and has permission from parents) to take the pet home at the end of the year? Even if the class decides that it is not a good idea to adopt a pet, the process of "caring" for the possible future pet will have been experienced in the process.

DAY 5

BELIEVING

Author Wayne Dyer writes about the impact that our beliefs have on our daily lives. Today, believe that you have all the resources to move your life in the direction of peace. Be aware of the simple, peaceful responses you receive.

QUOTES

For it is not enough to talk about peace.
One must believe in it.
And it isn't enough to believe in it.
One must work for it.

—Eleanore Roosevelt
Former U.S. First Lady, first chairman U.S. Human Right's Commission

To believe in the face of utter hopelessness, every article of evidence to the contrary, to ignore apparent catastrophe. We do it every day, I realized. We are so much stronger than we imagine, and belief is one of the most valiant and long-lived human characteristics.

—Lance Armstrong
Champion bicyclist and cancer survivor

QUESTIONS AND DEFINITIONS

1. What is a belief and how do beliefs affect our lives? Give examples.

2. How do beliefs affect the choices we make or don't make?

3. What are some beliefs you have about yourself? Other people? Life? Peace? How do these beliefs affect your choices?

4. How can your beliefs limit you? How can your beliefs empower you? What are some limiting or empowering beliefs that you have about yourself?

5. What is the role of beliefs (i.e., personal, religious, etc.) in the creation of conflict?

6. What are some beliefs held by heroes (in sports, science and health, human rights, music, labor and jobs, and other fields of endeavor) that have changed the world?

BELIEVING / ACTIVITIES

ACTIVITIES

 5.1 Break into small groups and role-play. What would it look like to completely believe in yourself and your abilities? Create an improvised scene depicting your life when you completely believe in yourself and your abilities. Perform these skits for the class.

 5.2 In triads, compare the differences between those areas of your life in which you believe in your abilities and those areas in which you doubt yourself. What differences do you see? How do your beliefs affect you? Where did those beliefs come from? Can you change them?

 5.3 What beliefs do you carry that impact your life regarding your experience of violence and nonviolence? What would you like to believe? How can you change your current belief system?

 5.4 Research and write a short story about a nonviolent hero (famous, local, someone in school or someone identified in a "courageous" activity). Write about what these individuals believed about themselves, their community, life and peace. How did the person's beliefs affect his or her choices, decisions and course of events?

 5.5 Decorate an I BELIEVE I CAN scroll. Have students remind themselves of their challenge areas. You can provide a special sheet of paper for them to create a scroll. Then, supply a length of ribbon to tie up the scroll. These can also be kept at school or given to students to keep in their rooms at home.

 5.6 This activity is a long-term project that extends the Art Activity above. Create an evaluation sheet to go home with the I BELIEVE I CAN scroll. Ask students to look at it once or twice a week during the *Season for Nonviolence*. Each time they look at the scroll they will record the date and time. They will also note what prompted them to look at the scroll at that moment and how it made them feel. Evaluate this experiment. Does practicing "belief" in yourself make you feel more peaceful and more nonviolent toward yourself? Does it help you reach your goals?

DAY 6

SIMPLICITY

"Live simply so that others may simply live." When Mohandas K. Gandhi retired his three-piece suit to wear a simple piece of cloth, he was demonstrating the principle of this statement in action. Today, do one thing for the sake of simplicity in your life. How will it render your world more peaceful?

QUOTES

It is vain to do with more, what can be done with less.

—William Occam

14th century philosopher

Simplicity of living, if deliberately chosen, implies a compassionate approach to life. It means that we are choosing to live our daily lives with some appreciation for the rest of the world.

—Duane Elgin

Author of *Voluntary Simplicity*, educator, media activist

QUESTIONS AND DEFINITIONS

1. What areas of your life seem complicated?

2. In what ways would you like to simplify your life?

3. If you had no money and needed a gift for someone you really cared about, what simple gift could you give them? What could you make? What could you do?

4. How does living more simply relate to a culture of nonviolence?

ACTIVITIES

 6.1 Role-play what it would be like to live without all the material objects you are used to. What would be simpler? What would be more complex? Would you be happier?

 6.2 How would it affect your life if there was no electricity for three days? What positive things could you do that don't cost money or require electricity? Explore ways in which young people from other cultures and in other times have/had fun in simple ways. What did your parents and grandparents do? Research and interview people about things that they do.

continued ▶

SIMPLICITY / ACTIVITIES, *continued*

 6.3 Make a special gift out of found or recycled items. Add your personal touch and ingenuity to make your gift special. To whom will you give this gift and why?

 6.4 Spend an afternoon learning the Quaker Song, "Tis a Gift to Be Simple." Singing together is a simple means of enjoyment and learning together on this topic.

 6.5 Research the life of Mahatma Gandhi. He went from wearing three piece suits, ties and a starched shirt to wearing a swath of draped cotton. Why? Check your library or search the Internet. How is your present day thinking impacted by the actions that Gandhi chose to take in his life?

DAY 7

EDUCATION

Knowledge strengthens your conviction and deepens your wisdom and understanding. Learn about the power of nonviolence by educating yourself. Read an article, periodical or book, or watch a video on a subject that relates to nonviolence. Learn about human rights, diversity, ecology, history, politics, forgiveness, spirituality, peace studies, biographies of heroes, and more.

QUOTES

We must remember that intelligence is not enough. Intelligence plus character—that is the goal of true education. The complete education gives one not only the power of concentration, but worthy objectives upon which to concentrate.

—Dr. Martin Luther King, Jr.

President and founder of the Southern Christian Leadership Conference

Education is the most powerful weapon that you can use to change the world.

—Nelson Mandela

First president of a desegregated South Africa (1918–)

And say, finally, whether peace is best preserved by giving energy to the government, or information to the people. This last is the most certain, and the most legitimate engine of government. Educate and inform the whole mass of the people. Enable them to see that it is their interest to preserve peace and order, and they will preserve them. They are the only sure reliance for the preservation of our liberty.

—Thomas Jefferson

Author of the Declaration of Independence (1743–1826)

I know of no safe repository of the ultimate power of society but the people. And if we think them not enlightened enough, the remedy is not to take the power from them, but to inform them by education.

—Thomas Jefferson

3rd U.S. President, founder of the Democratic Party, violinist

QUESTIONS AND DEFINITIONS

1. What would your life be like without an education? Does it make a difference? How?

2. What is something positive that you have learned that has really made a difference in your life?

3. How is the education you get from parents, teachers, and peers different?

4. What is the most important thing you have learned regarding nonviolence?

EDUCATION / ACTIVITIES

ACTIVITIES

 7.1 Begin a journal to record what you are learning about nonviolence. Include personal reflections, quotes, stories and biographies, important events, pictures, art, poems, etc. At the end of the *Season for Nonviolence*, show your journal to someone you love and with whom you would like to share the principles you have learned and the meaning that they have held for you.

 7.2 As a class, create a lesson on nonviolence that you can share with someone outside of school, perhaps a parent-education evening, or a visit to a scout troop. Debrief your teaching experience with the whole class.

 7.3 Describe and illustrate the most important lesson you have learned about how to neutralize violence. Who was the protagonist of the story and who was the antagonist? Where did the lesson come from? Was that lesson something someone said or something you discovered on your own as a result of your experience?

 7.4 Invite a guest speaker to make an educational presentation to the class about a topic related to the philosophy and practice of nonviolence in one's personal life, interpersonal relationships or in society.

 7.5 Show a video on nonviolent heroes, the civil rights movement, human rights or ecological awareness (i.e., *Eyes on the Prize*, by PBS Video, or *Free at Last*, by Teaching Tolerance). See Video Resources, pgs. 181-183.

 7.6.1 Research and visit Web sites that can help you learn about: 1) nonviolence and peace, and 2) social issues, e.g., child labor, environment, safe schools, hunger, homelessness, nuclear disarmament, death penalty, human rights, youth and human rights, child welfare, etc.

7.6.2 Find at least three (3) facts, two (2) inspirational quotes, and one (1) story that inspires you. Create a presentation: a one page newsletter, a radio broadcast, a report, a skit, etc.

DAY 8

HEALING

Writer, poet, activist, and professor Maya Angelou turned a traumatic childhood experience into a catalyst for creativity and achievement. Today, choose a painful incident in your life and find the "gift" it is "giving to you." Consciously share this gift with others.

QUOTES

Every time a seed has an occasion to manifest itself, it produces new seeds of the same kind... If we plant wholesome, healing, refreshing seeds, they will take care of the negative seeds, even without our asking of them...Healthy seeds function similarly to antibodies...Each of us needs a reserve of seeds that are beautiful, healthy, and strong enough to help us during difficult moments.

—Thich Nhat Hanh
Nobel Peace Prize nominee 1964

QUESTIONS AND DEFINITIONS

1. What does "healing" mean to you? What kinds of things need healing other than our physical body (e.g., personal, emotional, physical, community, national, etc.)?

2. Describe a healing experience from your life. How did it change things?

3. What can get in the way of healing?

4. How does anger affect the process of healing? How can anger be expressed in healthy, nonviolent ways?

5. What are some things people do to help themselves heal (music, writing, being quiet, sports, etc.)?

ACTIVITIES

 8.1 Choose a recent painful experience or event. How did it affect you? What is your potential for growth? What is the potential gift? What quality might you demonstrate in order to move on? Express this in a drawing.

continued ▶

HEALING / ACTIVITIES, *continued*

 8.2 Have students write out everything that needs to be healed in their lives. No one will be reading the paper so encourage everyone to write everything! Have a simple ceremony with a candle and a big aluminum tub of water. Allow each student to burn his or her paper and extinguish it in the tub of water as a symbol of his or her willingness to begin the healing. For the purposes of safety, instruct students to write along the very top of the page. Then twist the papers tightly. Students symbolically burn the tip of the paper where the words are written and drop it into the tub of water. (The facilitator should go first and explain safety precautions clearly.) **For mature students only.**

 8.3 Oprah Winfrey, Helen Keller, Rigoberta Menchu, Nelson Mandela, Thich Nhat Hanh, Magic Johnson and Mary K. Blige are examples of heroes and heroines who were able to heal their own lives by recognizing and accepting the "gift" within the pain. Choose a person from this list or someone else of your choice. Research and write about what you can learn from his or her story.

 8.4 Create a scenario to show how to heal hurt feelings, how to heal hurt relationships or how to heal communities. Introduce the characters and what happened that caused the problem. Then write a dialogue that demonstrates reconciliation and present it to the class.

DAY 9

DREAMING

Martin Luther King, Jr., had a great dream. What is your own dream for peace? Write it down. What is one thing you can do to honor your dream? Do it today.

QUOTES

What I treasure most in life is being able to dream. During my most difficult moments and complex situations, I have been able to dream a more beautiful future.

—Rigoberta Menchu Tum
Guatemalan Nobel Peace Laureate

Some men see things as they are and say, "Why?" I dream things that never were and say, "Why not?"

—Robert F. Kennedy
Former U.S. Attorney General, Presidential Candidate

QUESTIONS AND DEFINITIONS

1. **Share a dream that you have about your future.**

2. **Why are dreams important for us to have? How do dreams contribute to our lives?**

3. **How do dreams contribute to a nonviolent world? How do unfulfilled dreams contribute to violence? What are the ingredients one needs in order to fulfill a dream?**

4. **Is peace a dream? When you dream of peace, what does it look like?**

5. **How is a dream different from a commitment?**

6. **It is said that a goal is a dream with a deadline attached. What does this statement mean? Do you agree with it?**

ACTIVITIES

 9.1 Draw pictures of your personal dream of peace using pastels and watercolors. Then, write several steps you can take to make your dream of peace come true. Incorporate these thoughts into your drawing. What kind of person do you need to become? How will you know that the dream is realized? Hang these around the room to remind everyone of their intention and commitment.

continued ▶

DREAMING / ACTIVITIES, *continued*

ACTIVITIES

 9.2 Who is someone you admire who has made a positive contribution to your life, your community or your world? What is/was his or her dream? What qualities did that person develop that helped to fulfill the dream? What small steps did they take along the way? Write about this person and then write about a dream that you have. What is one thing you can do every day to honor your dream?

 9.3 Move the desks aside. Dim the lights. Have students lie down on their backs with their heads in the center of a circle or place chairs in a circle with backs to the center. Facilitator uses guided imagery to relax the group and take them on a journey to the "land of peace." What does it look like? What does it feel like? What are the children doing there? Share images that were revealed.

(Spinning Inward: Using Guided Imagery with Children for Learning, Creativity and Relaxation by Maureen Murdock. See Student Bibliography, page 178.)

 9.4 The quotes for today refer to different aspects of "dreaming" and the relationship of "dreaming" to the practice of nonviolence. The Langston Hughes quote talks about a dream not realized, the Rigoberto Menchu Tum quote talks about the hope found in dreams, and the Robert F. Kennedy quote talks about determination and action. Select an issue from current events and write a thought paper in relation to these three quotes.

DAY 10

FAITH

When César Chávez was organizing farm workers, he challenged them to say, "Sí, se puede" (Yes, it is possible.) when they didn't know how they would overcome obstacles. Today, say, "Yes, it is possible," even if you don't know how your goal will be realized. Have faith and say, "It is possible," until you find a way.

QUOTES

Faith consists in believing when it is beyond the power of reason to believe.

—Voltaire

17th century French philosopher, imprisoned and exiled for political opinions.

Let us consider the power of Faith, as demonstrated by one of the world's greatest souls, Mahatma Gandhi. In this man the world had one of the most astounding examples of the possibilities of Faith. Gandhi didn't have money, no home, no battleships, soldiers or any other material resources, yet he had more potential power than any man living in his time. How did he come by this power? He created it out of his understanding of the principle of Faith and through his leadership which inspired two hundred million people to move in unison, as a single mind. What other force on earth, except Faith, could do as much?

—Thomas Merton

Roman Catholic monk, author

…Faith is permanent, happiness and unhappiness are fleeting things.

—Mohandas K. Gandhi

Attorney, defeated the British Empire in India

Faith is the sense of life, that sense by virtue of which man does not destroy himself, but continues to live on. It is the force whereby we live.

—Leo Tolstoy

Russian author, philosopher (1818-1910)

QUESTIONS AND DEFINITIONS

1. What is faith?

2. In what ways do you have faith in yourself? In what ways do you demonstrate a lack of faith in yourself?

3. Think of two people you admire, who are heroes or heroines in history. In what did they have faith? How did their faith make a difference?

4. Name an area in your life in which you have faith. How does your faith enrich your life?

5. How do we hold on to faith when things go badly? What can we do to develop our faith?

FAITH / ACTIVITIES

ACTIVITIES

10.1 To demonstrate your faith, design nonviolence posters with the words: "It is possible!" included on them. Display them on campus.

10.2 Go to the library with your class. Find books and articles that tell stories of faith: peace leaders and humanitarians, athletes, strong individuals who have lived with handicaps (i.e., Christopher Reeve, Harriet Tubman, Helen Keller, Desmond Tutu, Anne Sullivan, Stephen Hawking). Have students give oral reports on these individuals and note similarities found in their ideas and life stories.

10.3 Pretend you are one of the heroes of nonviolence facing one of your greatest tests/challenges/crises. Write a diary entry describing how your faith supports you at this time.

10.4 Write an essay on a time in your life when your faith made a positive difference.

DAY 11

CONTEMPLATION

For at least three minutes, relax, breathe and let your mind be fed by "whatsoever is good and beautiful." Sacred scripture states, "As a man thinketh in his heart, so is he."

QUOTES

The man who sat on the ground in his tipi meditating on life and its meaning, accepting the kinship of all creatures and acknowledging unity with the universe of things was infusing into his being the true essence of civilization.

—Chief Luther Standing Bear
Chief of the Oglala Sioux, Brulé

QUESTIONS AND DEFINITIONS

1. **How is contemplation different from thinking? What are different ways to contemplate?**

2. **What kind of environment can you create to encourage a practice of daily contemplation in your life?**

3. **How does it feel to be alone with your thoughts?**

4. **How can the art of contemplation make a difference in your life?**

5. **How can contemplation keep you from over-reacting?**

6. **Can you sit in silence with friends? What happens in the silence? How do you feel?**

ACTIVITIES

 11.1 Take time to sit quietly in class together. See what thoughts come to mind. You may use music to help quiet and focus the class. Baroque slow movements have been proven to slow down the central nervous system. Students can bring music that they think would be good for contemplation.

 11.2 Practice deep breathing together. Breathe in to a count of four and out to a count of eight. Be silent on the "in breath" and make a "ssss" sound on the "out breath," this will help focus the class and keep them in present time.

continued ▶

CONTEMPLATION / ACTIVITIES, *continued*

 11.3 Contemplate on specific subjects such as the shape of our future, the most beautiful detail of your life, your strongest goal. When negative thoughts arise, substitute them with nurturing thoughts. Practice this in class.

 11.4 With appropriate music playing, create your own inner sanctuary—a place you can go to in your own mind that is peaceful, beautiful, safe and refreshing. While music plays, draw or write about your sanctuary. How does it feel, look, smell, taste?

 11.5 Pass out charcoal and pastel art supplies and paper. Do a silent/stillness meditation in which each student watches his or her own breath and the thoughts that move through his or her mind. When the class has settled into the process, you can read a contemplative passage on the idea of nonviolence. Then ask that the stillness be maintained while artwork is done, based on what came to mind during the meditation. Notice the variety of experiences that students have had in their lives with regard to non-violence and also which "experiences" come from the media and really aren't personal experiences at all. Help students distinguish the difference between their personal experience and what they have heard and accepted as their own about the idea, values and principles of nonviolence.

11.6 Do "quick writes" together. Suggest a word or topic and ask students to draw or write from their stream of consciousness—a free flow of drawing or writing without thinking about, analyzing or editing what comes out. Ask that this be done for five minutes without talking, stopping or asking for help. Ask volunteers to share their work. (Students are not required to share with the class.)

DAY 12

DISCIPLINE

The word discipline is a descendant of the word "disciple." It is the discipleship of the self. The only true and lasting discipline is self-discipline. Today, make time for coming into alignment with your full potential.

QUOTES

Success isn't measured by money or power or social rank. Success is measured by your discipline and inner peace.

—Mike Ditka
Pro Football Hall of Famer

Self-discipline is that which, next to virtue, truly and essentially raises one man above another.

—Joseph Addison
English political essayist and poet (1672–1719)

Self respect is the fruit of discipline; the sense of dignity grows with the ability to say no to oneself.

—Rabbi Abraham Joshua Heschel (1907-1972)
Activist, Professor of Jewish Ethics and Mysticism (1945–1972)

The hope of a secure and livable world lies with disciplined nonconformists who are dedicated to justice, peace and brotherhood.

—Martin Luther King Jr.
From *Strength to Love* (1929–1968)

QUESTIONS AND DEFINITIONS

1. **What are some different kinds of discipline?**

2. **In what area of your life or studies are you most disciplined?**

3. **How is discipline different from talent? How do they work together?**

4. **Can someone with discipline be successful without talent? Can someone with talent be successful without discipline? Why?**

5. **What does discipline have to do with discipleship?**

DISCIPLINE / ACTIVITIES

ACTIVITIES

 12.1 Make a list of all the activities that require personal discipline for you to do, even though you may feel good when you have completed them (i.e., doing the dishes, cleaning your room, sweeping the steps, working out, etc.). Once you have identified these areas, make an agreement with yourself during the *Season for Nonviolence*. What will you put in place to improve your self-discipline?

 12.2 Review Martin Luther King's "Letter from the Birmingham Jail," Gandhi's "Eight Blunders," the United Farm Workers Pledge, and/or other historic "pledges." of nonviolence for inspiration and ideas. Then brainstorm as a class to make a list of the disciplines related to the practice of nonviolence that you would pledge to practice.

 12.3 Choose a person who is an outstanding leader in his or her field. It could be an artist, athlete, activist, philosopher, entrepreneur, scientist or statesman. Research his or her life, and the role of discipline in fulfilling their goals. Include specific disciplines they employed. What part does discipline play in their mastery of each selected practice? **EXTRA CREDIT:** Find out what that person has to say about the role that discipline played in their successes.

DAY 13

CREATIVITY

The worst thing you can do to a human soul is to suppress its natural desire to create. Identify at least five ways in which you express your creativity everyday. Today, allow something unpredictable and joyous to express through you.

QUOTES

The first man to raise his fist is the man who has run out of ideas.

—H.G. Wells
English journalist, humanitarian, novelist known as the father of modern science fiction (1866-1946)

There is one thing stronger than armies of the world, and that is an idea whose time has come.

—Victor Hugo
French author (1802-1885)

Learn the craft of knowing how to open your heart and to turn on your creativity. There's a light inside of you.

—Judith Jamison
Dancer, director, Alvin Ailey Dance Co.

QUESTIONS AND DEFINITIONS

1. How does your creativity express through you (i.e., dance, poetry, cooking, etc.)?

2. What are some creative avenues you have not explored?

3. What types of things/activities enhance your creativity?

4. What types of things hinder your creativity?

5. How does your personal "inner critic" block your creative process?

6. How does creative expression contribute to a nonviolent culture?

ACTIVITIES

 13.1 Bring a box from home and decorate it with things that express who you are. Decorate the inside with thoughts and dreams, and decorate the outside with things that show how you physically express yourself in the world.

 13.2 Create something that expresses your experience of violence or nonviolence in your life.

continued ▶

CREATIVITY / ACTIVITIES, *continued*

 13.3 Choose a topic and write a class poem. Each student adds one line each by folding the paper after each written line. Each student sees only the line they write, and the line written directly above their own. One class representative reads the resulting poem.

 13.4 When and in what areas are you most creative? Write about your creativity, and about the most creative person you know and how that person inspires you. How are you like them? How can you express more of the creative part of you?

 13.5 Bring magazines and glue to class and have students create a collage that represents their hopes and dreams regarding a nonviolent world.

DAY 14

HUMILITY

Making mistakes is a part of learning and growing, simply an "error in approach." Today, freely acknowledge at least one mistake you have made and reflect for a couple of minutes on what you have learned.

QUOTES

Humility leads to strength and not to weakness. It is the highest form of self-respect to admit mistakes and to make amends for them.

—John J. McCloy

Assistant Secretary of State during WWII, nuclear disarmament advocate

I claim to be a simple individual liable to err like any other fellow mortal.
I own, however, that I have humility enough to confess my errors and to retrace my steps.

—Mahatma Gandhi

Father of active nonviolent resistance in the 20th Century

Pride is concerned with who is right. Humility is concerned with what is right.

—Ezra Taft Benson

Patriot, statesman, Secretary of Agriculture (1899-1944)

QUESTIONS AND DEFINITIONS

1. What is humility?

2. Some people associate humility with weakness. Some associate humility with strength. With what do you associate humility? Give examples.

3. How does making a mistake relate to the idea of humility? How can humility help us to learn and grow from our mistakes?

4. Is there such a thing as false humility? What forms does false humility take?

ACTIVITIES

 14.1 Choose partners and share a time with your partner when you made a serious mistake and learned a great lesson from it.

continued ▶

HUMILITY / ACTIVITIES, *continued*

 14.2 Describe a disagreement you observed between two people. What was each person's point of view? How could a little humility on the part of each person have made a difference? Role-play scenarios in which each person practices humility, or not being humble. How does humility affect the outcome of the disagreement? What opportunities does humility create?

 14.3 Take a class trip to the library and investigate the life of Johnny Appleseed, George Washington Carver or Rosa Parks. How did these individuals impact the world and how did their lives demonstrate humility?

 14.4 Imagine Gandhi before the English government in his very simple garments. Imagine Mandela just coming out of prison, meeting with the president of South Africa. Imagine Ruby Bridges facing isolation and discrimination at school. What can you learn from them about humility?

 14.5 Draw a picture of someone in your life or family who demonstrates a quality of humility. Share your drawing and why you chose that person.

DAY 15

REVERENCE

Environmentalist John Muir said, "Everybody needs beauty as well as bread, places to play in and pray in, where Nature may heal and cheer and give strength to body and soul." Today go for a walk and realize the beauty around, above and below you.

QUOTES

The cause of violence is not ignorance. It is self-interest...Only reverence can restrain violence— reverence for human life and the environment.

—William Sloan Coffin, Jr.

Yale University Chaplin, Civil Rights leader, peace activist

If a man loses his reverence for any part of life, he will lose his reverence for all of life.

—Albert Schweitzer

Humanitarian, missionary, medical doctor

It is along the path of reverence and obedience that the race has reached the goal of freedom, of self-government, of a higher morality, and a more abundant spiritual life.

—Calvin Coolidge

30th U.S. President (1871–1933)

A nation should be judged not by how it treats its highest citizens; but how it treats its lowest.

—Nelson Mandela

First President of free South Africa

We see that when the activities of life are infused with reverence, they come alive with meaning and purpose. We see that when reverence is lacking from life's activities, the result is cruelty, violence and loneliness.

—Gary Zukav

Author, U.S. Army Green Beret in Vietnam

QUESTIONS AND DEFINITIONS

1. In the practice of nonviolence, the standard we use to measure behavior is whether or not it holds a reverence for life.

2. How do we manifest the ideals represented in the quotes above, in our classroom, community, country, and individual lives?

continued ▶

R E V E R E N C E / QUESTIONS, *continued*

QUESTIONS AND DEFINITIONS

3. What are the things that you hold reverence for in your life (nature, music, people)? Why is it important to be reverent and how do you show that reverence? Demonstrate a way in which you express reverence.

4. How is reverence different from simple appreciation?

5. Did you ever see something so beautiful that it took your breath away?

6. How does reverence relate to the practice of nonviolence?

ACTIVITIES

 15.1 Create a three dimensional class scene (a diorama). Invite students to bring objects that symbolize things, events and ideas that they hold reverent in their lives. Students may share what the objects symbolize for them as they add it to the scene/diorama.

 15.2 Write about a holiday, event or time in history for which your family holds a special reverence. How do you celebrate or acknowledge it? What is the tone of the celebration or remembrance: celebratory, sad, etc.

 15.3 Design a three-paneled brochure meant to encourage the reader to hold a reverence for life. Select collage images and bold words that show aspects of life that you revere. On some portion of the brochure, select images that indicate a lack of reverence. Use this contrast to express your own views as well as to inform the reader.

 15.4 Create a class table of "Reverence for Life and Nonviolence." Bring in one object that symbolizes the gifts of the kind of life you wish for others you love.

 15.5 Write a letter to someone who is not yet born. Address your letter to an unborn niece, nephew, baby brother or sister, or imaginary future child. Use descriptive language and prose to describe your wishes for the kind of world you want them to have. Then tell them what you are willing to do in order to secure that future for them.

continued ▶

R E V E R E N C E / ACTIVITIES, *continued*

 15.6 Choose a rock, flower, tree or a special object to be your "partner" for this activity. Look at it silently for at least five minutes. Notice the small details, the colors, the lines and texture. Notice how you feel as you commune with your chosen "partner." Share the things you have noticed as you pass the object around the room. What did you discover about yourself in relationship to your "partner?"

 15.7 Research **The United Nations International Decade for a Culture of Nonviolence and Peace** (see page A6-A7). How does it demonstrate a reverence for life? Why do you think it is important? How do you think it is living up to the tenets (beliefs) of this document?

DAY 16

LEADERSHIP

Nonviolent leadership expresses integrity, courage, wisdom and vision that is meant for the highest good of all concerned. Where can you assume more leadership today?

QUOTES

You do not lead by hitting people over the head—that's assault, not leadership.

—Dwight D. Eisenhower

Commander of U.S. Armed Forces in Africa, called for
complete desegregation of U.S. Armed Forces, 34th U.S. President

If your actions inspire others to dream more, learn more, do more and become more, you are a leader.

—John Quincy Adams

6th President of the U.S., Civil Rights activist in the
House of Representatives, abolitionist

Time is neutral and does not change things. With courage and initiative, leaders change things.

—Reverend Jesse Jackson

Civil Rights activist, President of the Rainbow PUSH Coalition

The best soldier does not attack. The superior fighter succeeds without violence, the greatest conqueror wins without a struggle, and the most successful manager leads without dictation. This is called intelligent non-aggressiveness; this is called mastery of men.

—Lao-Tsu

Chinese Philosopher, father of Taoism and Tai Chi Chuan

QUESTIONS AND DEFINITIONS

1. Do you consider yourself to be a leader or a follower? Why? Do you believe that leadership can be cultivated? Must a person be a "born leader?"

2. Even if you do not unconditionally call yourself a leader, everyone possesses some quality of leadership. Identify at least one leadership quality that you possess. How will you develop it?

3. Brainstorm in class about the qualities and attributes of leadership. Who do you know who possesses those attributes? How have they influenced you?

4. Make a list of nonviolent leaders. What qualities do they have in common? What contributions have they made for the greater good? How were they rewarded or rejected by those around them?

LEADERSHIP / ACTIVITIES

ACTIVITIES

 16.1 Begin this activity with a warm-up exercise to unite and sensitize the group. Introduce the improvisational concept known as Moving Clump. A large open gymnasium or theatre space is needed. The class begins randomly, shoulder-to-shoulder, arms and legs free to move and change. Someone is selected to begin as the leader. The leader starts a sound and movement that the group will follow. As the clump explores space, sound, random action, direction and rhythm, new leadership should be allowed to emerge and change many times as the play continues. The facilitator may have to restart the exercise several times until the play begins to flow spontaneously. Debrief the exercise in terms of leadership and natural inclination.

 16.2 First, have student volunteers read aloud to the class chapters from *The Tao of Leadership: Leadership Strategies for a New Age* by John Heider. Have students read slowly to pay attention to the rhythm and qualities of the words and phrasing, from a poetic standpoint. Students should allow themselves to absorb the message through the musicality and the feelings as well as the words. Then have each student take one chapter and explore the meaning and efficacy of that chapter in a thought paper. Present these to the class. Allow these presentations to begin a dialogue and exploration of the Taoist view of leadership. How does it relate to our world today? How does it relate to the practice of nonviolence?

 16.3 Select an example of nonviolent leadership, either current or historic. Then research and develop an opinion paper to consider the actions and effectiveness of the individual leader or social movement for change on which you are reporting. If you think the leadership could have been more effective, explain how. If it was highly effective, consider why and how so?

 16.4.1 Divide the class into teams. Have each team take one of the following examples of leadership development and report on it to the class: the Highlander Research and Education Center, "popular education" as developed by Paulo Freire, and "Freedom Summer" in Mississippi, 1964. Provide a background and description of your example. What are the main ideas and values? Who were the leaders? Create a timeline. Have all members of your team take part in the research and presentation.

16.4.2 Debrief this project in terms of leadership in your group during the research and presentation development. How were decisions made? Who emerged as leader of your group? Do you know why? What qualities did they demonstrate?

 16.5 Long Term Project: Create a play reading in the style of an old radio show. Divide the class in half. One half will explore leaders who have used their power to serve and the other half will explore leaders who have abused their power. On each side have a two-person team report on each leader. One will report on the leader him- or herself, distinguishing values and qualities, the relationship with supporters and opposition, outcomes sought, and the legacy. The other will assume the identity of someone affected by the leader and the policy described, and tell his or her personal story. Debrief.

DAY 17

INTEGRITY

"Do the right thing." Film director Spike Lee used these words as a title for one of his movies. When faced with a choice today, listen to your conscience. You know what's right. Do it.

QUOTES

Nothing so completely baffles one who is full of trick and duplicity, than the straightforward and simple integrity in another.

—Charles Caleb Colton
Author, philosopher, statesman (1780-1832)

Integrity is doing the right thing, even if nobody is watching.

—Jim Stovall
Author, President of the Narrative Television Network

If you have integrity, nothing else matters. If you don't have integrity, nothing else matters.

—Albert Camus
French Existentialist author and philosopher (1913–1960)

Cowardice asks the question "Is it safe?"
Expediency asks the question, "Is it politic?"
Vanity asks the question, "Is it popular?"
But, conscience asks the question, "Is it right?"
And there comes a time when one must take a position that is neither safe, nor politic, nor popular, but one must take it because one's conscience tells one that it is right.
—Dr. Martin Luther King
President of Montgomery Improvement Association

QUESTIONS AND DEFINITIONS

1. How is integrity different from honesty?

2. Is integrity a quality that you can develop, or are you born with it?

3. How does your integrity influence your choices and decisions?

4. How do you know when something is right? What is the value of personal integrity?

5. How do you deal with a cashier who gives you too much change?

INTEGRETY / ACTIVITIES

ACTIVITIES

 17.1 Do the right thing! Make individual drawings or posters that show the outcome of two different choices made to respond to the same dilemma. Discuss the part that integrity plays in the different outcomes.

 17.2 Make a list of integrity choices that people in your age group are up against every day. In what way(s) do peers, the media and family influence these choices? Are you more likely to rely on your own integrity or follow your peer group? What does it require of you to stand in your own integrity?

 17.3 Write a short story about a time when you listened to your heart at the cost of sacrificing your popularity or your parents' approval in the process. You may exaggerate the consequences for dramatic effect. Use diagrams.

 17.4 Research the Pentagon Papers and the role that Daniel Ellsberg played in exposing them, or research another famous "whistle-blower." Write a thought paper and speculate about the part that integrity may have played in the choices that person made.

DAY 18

FREEDOM

Civil rights activist Diane Nash said, "Freedom, by definition, is people realizing that they are their own leaders." Take a leadership role today in your own life. Find one way you can be more expressive of who you truly are.

QUOTES

When people decide they want to be free, there is nothing that can stop them.

—Bishop Desmond Tutu

Anglican Archbishop Emeritus of Cape Town, South Africa
1984 Nobel Peace Prize Laureate, social activist

The truth is that we are not yet free; we have merely achieved the freedom to be free, the right not to be oppressed. We have not taken the final step of our journey, but the first step on a longer and more difficult road. For to be free is not merely to cast off one's chains, but to live in a way that respects and enhances the freedom of others. The true test of our devotion to freedom is just beginning. I've walked that long road to freedom. I have tried not to falter; I have made missteps along the way. But I have discovered that secret that after climbing a great hill, one only finds that there are many more hills to climb. I have taken a moment here to rest, to steal a view of the glorious vista that surrounds me, to look back on the distance I have come. But I can rest only for a moment, for with freedom come responsibilities, and I dare not linger, for my walk is not yet ended.

—Nelson Mandela

1993 Nobel Peace Prize Laureate

If you want to be free, there is but one way; it is to guarantee an equally full measure of liberty to all your neighbors. There is no other.

—Carl Schurz

Journalist, statesman, soldier, abolitionist, U.S. Senator (1829–1906)

The law will never make men free; it is men who have got to make the law free.

—Henry David Thoreau

Essayist, naturalist, author of the *Transcendentalist Movement*

There is nothing in all the world greater than freedom. It is worth paying for; it is worth losing a job for; it is worth going to jail for.

—Reverend Martin Luther King, Jr.

Nonviolent leader of the U.S. Civil Right's movement

Freedom without obligation is anarchy. Freedom with obligation is democracy.

—Earl Riney

American clergyman (1885–1955)

FREEDOM / QUESTIONS

QUESTIONS AND DEFINITIONS

1. What does it mean to be free?

2. Is there a difference between freedom and license? Explain.

3. What is the relationship between freedom and responsibility?

4. Can you be in a prison of your own making?

5. How can you be "free" in prison?

6. How do you experience freedom within structures, laws, rules, guidelines?

7. In your opinion, do you have too much or too little freedom?

ACTIVITIES

 18.1 Look through magazines and create a collage of pictures and words that express the idea of freedom to you. Write a sentence or two about the picture, relating it to freedom.

 18.2 Research what Victor Frankel (Holocaust survivor), Nelson Mandela, Mahatma Gandhi, Martin Luther King, Jr. and other leaders of nonviolence have to say about freedom.

 18.3 Have your class divide into three groups. Have each one create a framework for a government with freedom for all. Compare and contrast what you came up with. How difficult or easy was the process?

 18.4 Review the history of the United States of America and create a timeline of milestones of Freedom in our country. The class can be divided into groups for different time periods or include timelines of freedom from other cultures as well.
(A People's History of the United States by Howard Zinn. See Adult Bibliography, page 173)

 18.5 Write a first-person fictional story of an individual who participated in a freedom movement. Based on historical fact about the movement and time period, develop this character's story. You may choose to be on either side of the issue: how did your character participate or not and why? What happened? How did it feel to be a part of history? Share stories with the class.

18.6 Create a line chart on the board with No Control on the lowest end of the chart and Total Control on the top of the chart. Let each student enter his or her name on the continuum, and justify where they placed themselves. Debrief in terms of how and why students differ in their understanding of their own freedoms. What factors play into their loss or gain of freedom?

DAY 19

ACCEPTANCE

"Resentment, fear, criticism, and guilt cause more problems than anything else," says Louise Hay. Today, choose not to judge yourself (your looks, your capabilities, your expression). See yourself as unique, loving, capable and bright!

QUOTES

...grant me the serenity to accept the things I cannot change; the courage to change the things I can; and the wisdom to know the difference.

—Reinhold Niebur

excerpt, The Serenity Prayer

Attitude is your acceptance of the natural laws, or your rejection of the natural laws.

—Jim Rohn

Author, philosopher

QUESTIONS AND DEFINITIONS

1. Compare and contrast acceptance vs. tolerance. (Do you want to be accepted or tolerated?) How can acceptance lead to inclusivity?

2. How do resentment, fear, criticism and guilt affect people? How can they contribute to violence (to the self or others)? What gets in the way of letting go of these feelings?

3. Describe the relationship between self acceptance and accountability. How can we accept ourselves and be motivated to improve ourselves?

4. What are some thoughts about yourself and your life with which you can choose to be more accepting?

5. Does accepting yourself lead to accepting others? How?

ACTIVITIES

 19.1 Explain in essay form, discuss or create an art project depicting ways in which you have or have not been accepted by others and how it has affected you.

 19.2 Write an acceptance speech about yourself in the third person. Accept your challenges along with your strengths.

continued ▶

ACCEPTANCE / ACTIVITIES, *continued*

 19.3 Write 20 positive traits about yourself and share them with a friend, classmate or one other person.

 19.4 Free-hand draw a picture of what you would look like if you could completely accept yourself for who you are. What would be different? What would be the same? What sorts of things would it enable you to do?

 19.5 How we speak can heal criticism, judgment and guilt. Write down ways in which you criticize yourself. How can you acknowledge these opportunities for growth in a more positive way? For example, eliminate "never," "always," "should," and "can't" from your vocabulary.

Rather than:	Try:
"I keep making the same mistake."	"I am still learning how to…"
"I am so stupid!"	"I am developing my ability to…"
"I can't speak in front of groups."	"I intend to become more confident speaking to groups of people."

After the facilitator has introduced the skill, break up into groups of three and coach one another in re-creating more empowering and self-accepting ways of describing your opportunities for growth.

 19.6 In what way(s) do you feel acceptance can create peace between nations? Research two feuding countries. Examine their issues and write your own opinions regarding two or three major areas in which each country might practice acceptance.

DAY 20

SELF-FORGIVENESS

When you judge yourself, you tend to believe that who you are is what you have done or not done, what you have or don't have. Knowing that who you are is greater than all these things, today, forgive yourself for forgetting the good that is in you.

QUOTES

Forgiveness starts in our own hearts. Only when we have forgiven ourselves can we give it to, or receive it from others.

—Paul Ferrini
Minister, author, expert on forgiveness

It isn't until you come to a spiritual understanding of who you are...not necessarily a religious feeling, but deep down, the spirit within...that you can begin to take control.

—Oprah Winfrey
Producer, talk-show host, humanitarian

There is a place inside each of us that is more than our experiences, our deeds, and the circumstances and conditions of our lives. When we forgive ourselves, we are remembering that place of goodness and wholeness within us, and we begin to make new choices for our lives.

—Eisha Mason
Writer, visionary, co-author of *64 Ways to Practice Nonviolence*

QUESTIONS AND DEFINITIONS

1. How does self-forgiveness relate to the practice of nonviolence?

2. Have you ever consciously forgiven yourself for something specific?

3. What self-judgments have you made that might keep you from realizing your full potential? Can self-forgiveness transform self-judgment into wisdom? How?

4. How does the self-judgment you feel keep you from moving on?

5. What are some of the thoughts and feelings that get in the way of self-forgiveness?

6. What is the relationship between self-forgiveness and accountability (making amends)?

7. What does self-forgiveness look like and feel like?

SELF-FORGIVENESS / ACTIVITIES, *continued*

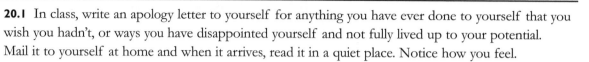
ACTIVITIES

20.1 In class, write an apology letter to yourself for anything you have ever done to yourself that you wish you hadn't, or ways you have disappointed yourself and not fully lived up to your potential. Mail it to yourself at home and when it arrives, read it in a quiet place. Notice how you feel.

20.2 Write an essay about the last thing you did that you wish you hadn't or that made you feel guilty later. If you had understood the consequences, would you have acted differently? How?

20.3 Identify an area of your life or an action you took that requires self-forgiveness. Describe how you feel about it. Then develop your own set of steps to self-forgiveness. What will you do? How will it work?

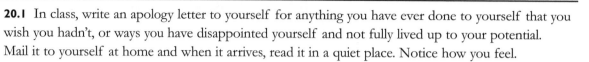
20.4 Divide the class into groups of four or five students. Let each group develop a ritual to signify personal self-forgiveness that can be expressed in community. Present ritual idea to the class and let the class select the one that feels most powerful. Then plan and perform the ritual together.

DAY 21

INSPIRATION

Think of at least two people who exemplify the practice of nonviolence. What do you admire about them? Practice these behaviors today so that other people may be inspired.

QUOTES

Enthusiasm is the inspiration of everything great.

—Christian Nevell Bovee
Author (1820-1904)

All of my activities run into one another and they have their rise in my insatiable love of mankind.

—Mohandas Gandhi
Humanitarian leader

Opportunities to find deeper powers within ourselves come when life seems most challenging.

—Joseph Campbell
Author, scholar on myths and comparative religion

Far and away the best prize that life has to offer is the chance to work hard at work worth doing.

—Theodore Roosevelt
26th U.S. President, Nobel Peace Prize for Mediation on
Russo-Japanese War (1820–1904)

QUESTIONS AND DEFINITIONS

1. What and who inspires you and why?

2. How do you know that you are inspired?

3. Is inspiration a function of the head or the heart?

4. If you were truly inspired, what could you accomplish and how would you do it?

5. How would you like to inspire others?

INSPIRATION / ACTIVITIES

ACTIVITIES

21.1.1 Visualize yourself at the Person of the Year awards. People who receive this award are a great inspiration to others. Where is the event held? Describe the venue and what it is like.

21.1.2 Someone who inspires you is giving the speech introducing the recipient of this year's award and the specific reasons why they are being honored in this way. Who is speaking and what are they saying about you?

21.1.3 You come forward to receive your award. How do you feel? What are you wearing? What does your award look like? What do you have to share with others in your awards speech? How does the audience respond?

21.1.4 Set up the classroom to enact the awards ceremony. Let students play the famous presenters. Let students receive an award or certificate. Let them read their speech and receive applause. Take Polaroid photos and make a poster. Let students keep the pictures of themselves.

21.2 Identify inspirational people you know who stand for nonviolence. What are the qualities they possess. Which of those qualities do you possess and which qualities are you willing to cultivate?

21.3 Give students a piece of paper and let them choose two or three crayons. Put on some inspirational music. Let everyone close their eyes and listen for five minutes. Then, with their eyes still closed, let students color the page, inspired by the feeling the music evokes. When they open their eyes, let them add words or phrases to the color that speak to inspiration and further define the drawing. Display the drawings to stay inspired.

DAY 22

MISSION

"My life is my message," said Gandhi. Write down what you want to stand for in your life. Note at least one way you can show, through action, that you stand for your beliefs. Take this action today.

QUOTES

Determine that the thing can and shall be done, and then we shall find the way.

—Abraham Lincoln

Considered the single most influential figure in the development of the United States of America

QUESTIONS AND DEFINITIONS

1. What is the difference between a mission and a goal?

2. When was the last time you were on a mission?

3. Name some historical figures who were really on life missions (from Hitler to Mother Teresa). Discuss the qualities that you attribute to these people.

4. What is a mission statement?

5. What is the message of your life based on the evidence of your choices, attitudes and actions?

6. How can someone tell when you are living your mission?

ACTIVITIES

22.1 Use the writing process to have students write a personal living mission statement or pledge. (You may want to read Thich Nhat Hanh's "Five Point Living Pledge" found at www.plumvillage.org.) Choose 5-10 of the personal qualities in this guide that you determine are most important to your practice.

22.2 After students have written a personal life mission statement, let them produce individual artistic documents with a place for the writer's signature and the signature of a witness. In dyads, give students an opportunity to share and witness each other's commitments and documents.

continued ▶

MISSION / ACTIVITIES, *continued*

 22.3 Write a class mission statement that applies to the practice of nonviolence at school and in the community. Make sure only to include items on which everyone can agree. Create a class scroll or a scroll for the entire school and let everyone sign it. Read it every day during the campaign.

 22.4 Choose a project or activity that would make your school a better place, and would symbolize a commitment to your class mission statement. Plan and take the steps to carry out your project.

DAY 23

PRAYER

"Prayer from the heart can achieve what nothing else in the world can," said Gandhi. Begin and end the day with a prayer for peace. Let peace begin with you.

QUOTES

Prayer is simply a way of probing our connection to the forces behind the world, whatever anyone may wish to call them. Maybe we pray to ourselves; maybe we pray to the intelligence behind nature; maybe prayer is just a way of discovering some of our own hopes and fears.

—Bo Lozof

From *It's A Meaningful Life*

The Prayer lends a new life to the day, binding it into the rhythmn of a sacred circle. Like a waterwheel that ceaselessly catches water out of a stream and spills it into a garden. The Prayer lifts us up again out of our preoccupations and sets us into sacred time. The Prayer empowers us to put aside ten thousand cares and realign to the unity and blessedness intrinsic to all things.

—Coleman Barks and Michael Green

From *The Illuminated Prayer*

Prayer itself is the central act of faith. It has its own promptings—a tenderness on the world's edge, a sense of need, some home-yearning of the soul. It is its own venture.

—George A. Buttrick

From *Prayer*

QUESTIONS AND DEFINITIONS

1. What does the word "prayer" suggest to you?

2. Discuss the various ways people pray, including spoken prayer, silent contemplation, meditation, abstinence and reciting hymns and scripture. What are other forms of prayer that you recognize?

3. Do you have to be affiliated with a specific religious group in order to pray?

4. When was the last time, if ever, you prayed in your heart for something or someone special? Did it change the outcome? Did it change the way you felt? How?

5. How does prayer relate to nonviolence? Does it surprise you that peace and civil rights movements often begin in spiritual communities? Why or why not?

PRAYER / ACTIVITIES

ACTIVITIES

 23.1 Assign students to research and bring in prayers of peace from different spiritual traditions. Sources can include their own family traditions, children's anthologies of peace writings, prayers for the earth, or collections of spiritual poetry and prose. Read them in class and let the students choose their favorites. Create a class ceremony and include many of these readings to experience the universality of prayers for peace.

 23.2 Ask students to write their own private prayer for peace. Ask them to write it as if they knew that anything written down is guaranteed to come to pass. Ask them to use their creativity to describe the best and most peaceful world they each can realize. Then have them decorate their personal peace prayer and keep it close to their hearts. Teachers can ask if anyone would like to share his or her prayer with the class.

 23.3 Draw individual pictures with scenes depicting world peace. What would this world look like? Create a class mural with your favorites scenes. Have everyone work on it together. When it is finished, recognize it as a prayer in action for the kind of world students want to create.

 23.4 Think about a troubled situation that you really care about (personal, community, school, worldwide). Write an affirmation for peace in that situation, include what it would take to make it work. Is this a "prayer?" Why or why not?

INTERPERSONAL

In order to create a peaceful world, we must learn

to practice nonviolence with one another.

DAY 24

HARMONY

Choosing not to engage in any form of gossip today contributes to harmony. Today, choose to see the good in yourself and others rather than finding fault.

QUOTES

If there is light in the soul, there will be beauty in the person. If there is beauty in the person, there will be harmony in the house. If there is harmony in the house, there will be order in the nation. If there is order in the nation, there will be peace in the world.
—Chinese Proverb

Always aim at complete harmony of thought and word and deed. Always aim at purifying your thoughts and everything will be well.
—Mohandas K. Gandhi
> Known as Mahatma, he often fasted as a nonviolent action and for personal repentance

The world is not to be put in order; the world is order incarnate. It is for us to harmonize with it.
—Henry Miller
> American writer

QUESTIONS AND DEFINITIONS

1. What is the meaning of harmony? How does it feel, look, and sound?

2. Describe the idea of harmony as it relates to an individual, a family, a community, the earth.

3. How do *you* know when things are in harmony?

4. What is required to foster greater harmony in your community, class, school, family, club, etc.? What steps can you take?

5. Does maintaining harmony mean accepting and keeping silent in the midst of injustice?

ACTIVITIES

 24.1 Study the poster print of The Peaceable Kingdom. Let the students share what they notice. How does harmony relate to nonviolence?

continued ▶

HARMONY / ACTIVITIES, *continued*

24.2 Let's talk about gossip. What's your experience with gossip—as one who spreads gossip or as one who has been affected by gossip? Why do people gossip? What if our gossip shared only positive things about someone? Break into dyads. Write positive gossip statements about your partner. Exaggerate, ham it up and gossip about your partner as you share these positive statements! Does this exercise create more harmony in your class?

24.3 Sing a simple song in unison. Then sing it in rounds that are in harmony. Which is more interesting? And why? What is required of the group to sing in harmony?

24.4 Play some harmonious music and allow the students to walk randomly around the room and gently "high five" or "low five" each other. Decide which one as you approach without speaking and change randomly. See how easy it can be to communicate and act harmoniously in this simple nonverbal way.

24.5 Decide on three areas in your life that could be more harmonious. What steps are you willing to take to be an agent of more harmonious interaction in those areas? Share with the class.

24.6 Some people said that civil rights activists were responsible for creating disharmony through their nonviolent civil disobedience. King and his followers said that they were merely calling attention to the disharmony (violence) that was already present. What did they mean by this? Read the *Letter From A Birmingham Jail* by Dr. Martin Luther King. Prepare notes and plan a debate to encourage class discussion on this issue.

DAY 25

FRIENDLINESS

To humorist Will Rogers, strangers were simply friends he hadn't met. View those you encounter today in that light. Make a new acquaintance.

QUOTE

The best way to destroy an enemy is to make him a friend.
—Abraham Lincoln
11th U.S. President, wrote the Emancipation Proclamation

QUESTIONS AND DEFINITIONS

1. Who is the friendliest person you know? How do you know it?

2. Is friendliness a quality you are born with or can you cultivate it?

3. Do you know a friendly stranger? How did they act and who are they?

4. How can you be a more friendly person?

5. Discuss the difference between friendliness and friendship? How are they different? How do they relate?

ACTIVITIES

 25.1 Listen to the songs *Bridge Over Troubled Water* or *Stand by Me*. Analyze and describe the lyrics, and listen again. Note the use of melody, tempo, and tone to relay the feelings of the message.

 25.2 Partner students randomly (preferably with someone they don't know well) and have them interview each other about friendship. Possible interview questions: Who is a good friend of yours? What do you like about that person? What makes him or her a special friend? What are several qualities that this person possesses that you appreciate?

 25.3 Have students create personal 3x5 trading cards with a picture and vital statistics about themselves. When they are finished, share them with the class and encourage students to trade them with people they would like to know better.

continued ►

FRIENDLINESS / ACTIVITIES, *continued*

25.4 Make cotton friendship bracelets and take a field trip to a senior center and give them to the residents, or sell them on campus and give the money to a local charity. Write a letter to introduce yourself to the recipient of your bracelet.

25.5 Have your class adopt a community elder (e.g., crossing guard or neighbor). Invite them to your classroom for tea and tell each other stories about your lives. How does learning about another person relate to the practice of nonviolence?

25.6 Experiment with friendliness on a class field trip to the mall. Choose some friendly acts and try them out on strangers, such as opening doors or allowing someone to take your place in line. Debrief about the ways in which individuals responded and how it made you feel.

DAY 26

RESPECT

Gandhi taught, "Language is an exact reflection of the character and growth of its speakers." Today, respect yourself and others by choosing not to use any profanity or "put downs."

QUOTES

"No one can make you feel inferior without your consent."
—Eleanor Roosevelt
Humanitarian and human rights advocate,
First Lady to President Franklin Delano Roosevelt

It is not our purpose to become each other; it is to recognize each other, to learn to see the other and to honor him for what he is.
—Herman Hesse
German/Swiss pacifist, author

QUESTIONS AND DEFINITIONS

1. What is respect and how do you show it to strangers?

2. Make a list of words we call each other that show respect, and words that show lack of respect. Which words do you hear most often? How do they make you feel?

3. Does a show of respect mean that you have to agree?

4. Is there a type of person that does not deserve your respect?

5. Does the development of self-respect increase your ability to respect others? How?

ACTIVITIES

 26.1 Draw a picture of someone for whom you have a great deal of respect. Frame the pictures with words that describe this person.

 26.2 Make a list of ways in which you can show respect to your peers, your parents, your school, your planet and yourself. Think of small ways and think of large ways. Even if you can't do them all right away, write down as many ideas as you can. Be specific and thorough.

continued ▶

RESPECT / ACTIVITIES, *continued*

 26.3 What feels disrespectful to you? After some discussion, each person gets to complete this sentence about disrespectful words, "One thing I never want to hear again is _____." Participants can also write their "put down" and, as they share it, throw it in the trash. As part of the ceremony, the facilitator takes the bag of trash to the dumpster. (Do not leave it in the room.)

 26.4 Agree to speak with complete respect to one another for the whole day. When you are spoken to respectfully say, "Thank you for your kind words." When you are spoken to in a way that feels disrespectful, make note of it, and do not respond. Discuss this exercise at the end of the day.

 26.5 Have each student select a different culture or a different period of time and explore ways in which that culture showed respect to others. You may refer to laws, language and tones of voice, facial expressions, greetings, body language and dress. Have students develop skits in which these differences are highlighted and which may either inform each other or dismay and cause confusion.

DAY 27

GENEROSITY

Mother Teresa said, "There is a hidden poverty more pervasive than lack of money. It is the poverty of the heart." Today, find three ways to generously give of your time, attention and resources to others.

QUOTES

We make a living by what we get, but we make a life by what we give.
—Sir Winston Churchill
Prime Minister of England (1874-1965)

Real generosity is doing something nice for someone who will never find out.
—Frank A. Clark
Photographer, artist (1865-1937)

Real education should educate us out of self into something far finer; into a selflessness which links us with all humanity.
—Lady Nancy Astor
English politician, first woman to sit on England's House of Commons

QUESTIONS AND DEFINITIONS

1. How can you be generous when you have no money?

2. What is true "generosity of the spirit?"

3. When was the last time you experienced yourself being truly generous?

4. Not including money, what was the most generous act or gift you ever received?

ACTIVITIES

 27.1 Make a list of all the toys you have outgrown. Have a toy drive at school and donate what you collect to a children's center. Or simply visit the center as a class. Spend time playing with and reading to the children.

 27.2 Make a gift certificate for your mom or dad, offer them a free car wash, a coupon to have the living room vacuumed or some other simple surprise gift that will make their day. What will you receive in return?

continued ▶

GENEROSITY / ACTIVITIES, *continued*

 27.3 Be generous to your school. Think of something that would make your campus a better or more beautiful place. Plan a fundraiser and follow through with it. The spirit of giving is contagious.

 27.4 Explore the world of philanthropy. Use the Internet to research organizations that do philanthropic work in your community. Interview a staff member to discover how they got started and what inspired them. Which of Gandhi's "Eight Blunders" on page A13 relate to the practice of philanthropy?

DAY 28

LISTENING

Today, stop what you are doing and take five minutes to listen to the feelings behind someone's words to you. Be fully present for the conversation and be interested in what the person is saying.

QUOTES

…One of the things which most deeply impressed me about the late A.J. Muste was his ability to listen with respect to those with whom he deeply disagreed, not as a tactic but because he hoped to catch in their remarks some truth he himself had missed.

—David McReynolds

War Resister League

Above all he learned how to listen with a still heart, with a waiting open soul, without passion, and without desire, without judgment, without opinions.

—Herman Hesse

Author of *Siddhartha*

So when you are listening to somebody, completely, attentively, then you are listening not only to the words, but also to the feeling of what is being conveyed, to the whole of it, not part of it.

—Jiddu Krishnamurti

Indian Philosopher, author (1895-1986)

Listening well is as powerful a means of communication and influence as to talk well!

—John Marshall

Chief Justice of the Supreme Court,
established landmark decision of Judicial Review (1755-1835)

An enemy is one whose story we have not heard.

—Gene Knudsen Hoffman

Quaker Peace activist

QUESTIONS AND DEFINITIONS

1. What is the difference between hearing something and listening to something?

2. Who really listens to you? Who do you really listen to?

3. How does it change your feeling about someone when they truly hear and understand your point of view, even if their opinion is different in the end?

4. Do you listen with your ears or your heart?

LISTENING / ACTIVITIES

ACTIVITIES

 28.1 Sit face to face with a partner at a distance that is comfortable for both of you. Listen for several moments with your eyes. Discuss how listening relates to the idea of nonviolence.

 28.2 What do you want from the person who is supposed to be listening to you? Make a list. Now evaluate yourself as a listener based on the list you have made. How are you willing to improve your listening?

 28.3 In groups of twos, partners take turns, each partner talking for several minutes while the other listens but does not speak. When the speaker is complete, the listener responds, "Thank you." Then have the listener tell back what they heard and notice if the whole message was conveyed and understood. Switch roles. Debrief. How did you experience yourself as the listener? How much care did you bring to listening? Were you able to hear any messages "in between the words?" As the speaker, what about the person's listening did you value? What was it like to have someone hear you accurately—or not? Were you able to listen and hear your own thoughts more clearly in the listener's silence?

 28.4 Share a piece of music sung in different languages. Discuss what was heard and what was felt through the listening.

DAY 29

FORGIVENESS

When we forgive, we do not condone hurtful behavior. When we realize that there is something within us that is more important than this wounding experience, we are free to let go of the past and move on with our lives. Today, write a letter to forgive someone. You do not have to mail it.

QUOTES

The weak can never forgive. Forgiveness is the attribute of the strong.

—M. K. Gandhi

Known as Mahatma or Great Soul

spent 2,338 days in prison for political views and social activism

Forgiving is not forgetting, it is letting go of the hurt.

—Mary McLeod Bethune

Founder of National Council of Negro Women (1854-1955)

When we forgive, we free ourselves from the bitter ties that bind us to the one who hurt us.

—Claire Frazier-Yzaguirre, MFT

Author, expert on forgiveness

Not to forgive is to be imprisoned by the past, by old grievances that do not permit life to proceed with new business. Not to forgive is to yield oneself to another's control ... to be locked into a sequence of act and response, of outrage and revenge, tit for tat, escalating always. The present is endlessly overwhelmed and devoured by the past. Forgiveness frees the forgiver. It extracts the forgiver from someone else's nightmare.

—Lance Morrow

Times columnist on national affairs

QUESTIONS AND DEFINITIONS

1. Is forgiveness something that you can make happen?

2. When you forgive someone, does it relieve them of responsibility for what they said or did? Discuss your point of view.

3. How can lack of forgiveness for yourself or for others hurt you?

4. Is forgiveness something you can do without involving another person?

5. When was the last time you were forgiven by someone? How did it make you feel? How did they let you know?

6. What would you have to know about yourself in order to forgive another person?

ACTIVITIES

 29.1.1 Experiment with steps to forgiveness. Reflect on an issue or a person that is difficult for you to forgive. What are the elements of the infraction? What do you want? Write a letter to your adversary. Include everything you want to say. Include your own responsibility for what happened. You will not be mailing this letter.

29.1.2 Have the class create a ceremony in which these letters can be destroyed as a way of letting go of animosity. Students can imagine a cord connecting them to their adversaries. Then symbolically cut the cord as the letters are destroyed to signify the forgiveness work you have done during this experiment. Debrief in terms of effectiveness. What did you learn? Did the process help you forgive? Did you learn anything about yourself?

 29.2 Research and learn about the mission of the Truth and Reconciliation Commission in South Africa and other countries. Select an event in history and hold a mock Truth and Reconciliation Commission. Who are key players? What needs to be healed?
(Refer to: New World Outlook, July–Aug. 1999, http://gbgm-umc.org/now/99jw/different.html and the book, *No Future Without Forgiveness* by Bishop Desmond Tutu. See video and Bibliography Resources.)

 29.3 Draw a picture of someone you have been unable to forgive. See if you can remember their good qualities. What, if anything, would be worth preserving in the relationship? If there is nothing worth regaining, can forgiveness still happen in you and how will it serve you?

DAY 30

AMENDS

Make amends today! Apologize to someone you may have hurt. Acknowledge your responsibility in the situation. What must you relinquish to make amends? What are the gains?

QUOTE

Humility leads to strength and not to weakness. It is the highest form of self-respect, to admit mistakes and to make amends for them.

—John (Jay) McCloy
Assistant Secretary of State during WWII,
nuclear disarmament advocate

QUESTIONS AND DEFINITIONS

1. What does it mean to "make amends?"

2. Is it enough to say, "I'm sorry?"

3. In what ways might making amends affect the person (you) making amends? How does pride factor in? How does the principle of nonviolence, which says, "hate the deed and not the doer," relate?

4. What are some of the things people commonly do to hurt each other? What kinds of things can one do to make amends?

5. When was the last time you made amends? How and what did you do?

ACTIVITIES

 30.1 Write a letter apologizing to someone you may have hurt. Explain what happened. Include principles that will help you effectively make amends: a) acknowledge what happened, b) take full responsibility for your part in what happened, c) apologize for what happened, and d) share your intention for the future regarding your behavior and the particular situation or relationship. Use varied sentence structure, precise vocabulary, appropriate tense and punctuation to maintain clarity of communication. Share some of these letters in class to hear which types of communication work best. Review effective ways of communicating.

 30.2 Work in partners and share with your partner something you think you did that may have hurt someone else. Let your partner role-play so that you can practice making amends to the person you think you have hurt. The partner is to listen and respond sincerely, as if he or she were the person hurt. Discuss how easy or difficult this was and how realistic the response seemed. What do you believe the outcome could be if world leaders would apply this practice? Include the four principles from activity 30.1 above.

continued ▶

AMENDS / ACTIVITIES, *continued*

 30.3 Make amends to someone you have hurt. Write about your experience.

 30.4 Use the Internet to learn about Restorative Justice and its effectiveness. To get started, check out "What is Restorative Justice?" *www.restorativejustice.org.*

 30.5 What do you think about restorative justice as an alternative to punishment? What kinds of offenses can you identify and what kind of restitution could be applied, to provide restorative justice in your community? How could you apply restorative justice to a situation for which you are responsible? Make a plan and carry it out. Write a news article about what happened.

DAY 31

CONFLICT RESOLUTION

True conflict resolution requires dialogue, effective listening, understanding and a willingness to create a new possibility and stay in the conversation until a resolution is achieved. Today, use conflict as an opportunity to learn something new about yourself and your adversary.

QUOTE

It is a conviction that war is not an answer to human conflict any more than cannibalism is to human hunger.

—**Bruce Kent**

International Peace Bureau president

QUESTIONS AND DEFINITIONS

1. The Chinese symbol for "conflict" is a combination of "crisis" and "opportunity."

   Define conflict and resolution. Are there negative and positive aspects of conflict? Give examples of the negative potential and the positive potential of conflict.

2. Can resolution ever be achieved by force? Can it be sustained by force? Why or why not? How?

3. What communication "blunders" hinder the peaceful resolution of conflict? What mistakes do you make? What mistakes have you observed others make?

4. Who in the public eye can you identify that facilitates the peaceful resolution of conflict by the ways in which he or she speaks about others, or to others?

5. What are examples of communication that you have witnessed in the media that undermine the peaceful resolution of conflict?

ACTIVITIES

31.1 Brainstorm examples of conflicts in four categories: personal/internal conflicts, everyday/external conflicts, local/legal conflicts and national/global conflicts. Can you think of other categories? Divide a piece of paper into two columns. List examples of each type of conflict and what a corresponding resolution might be.

continued ▶

R E S O L U T I O N / ACTIVITIES, *continued*

 31.2 Review what you have already learned about nonviolence. As a class, generate your own steps for resolving conflict based on the *64 Ways*. Be sure to honor feelings as well as address facts in the process. Then test your system the next time a conflict arises in class. Have the group work together to facilitate successful conflict resolution among its members. For homework, have each student write a thought paper about how effective the process was. What will you do again that worked? What will you alter? Revise and improve your system for next time.

 31.3 Create a conflict journal to raise your awareness of the conflicts you face everyday and how you handle them. Create and organize your journal in a way that can be used as both an assessment tool and an artistic representation of how you look at conflict and its resolution in your own life. What do you observe? Evaluate your own listening skills, willingness to compromise, dialogue skills and ability to grow.

 31.4 Research and list at least five local and/or national conflict resolution resources. Write a short paper about the origins of these programs and the basic elements of each. Who provided leadership in the developmental stages? Upper school students may want to compare and contrast programs and to speculate on their efficacy.

 31.5 Research ways that different countries have managed conflict. What kinds of consequences did the different solutions create? Write a case study and present it to the class. Compare and contrast the effectiveness and success of different approaches. Have students report on both violent and nonviolent attempts to solve conflict.

 31.6 Have the class select a current or historic event to explore. Hold a debate about different solutions to the conflict. Have some students debate the side opposite of their personal beliefs. What did the class learn from this experience? Did they come to understand another point of view? Did anyone change his or her mind? Why?

DAY 32

PATIENCE

According to Cesar Chavez, "Nonviolence is not inaction. It is hard work. It is the patience to win." When your plans seem delayed, choose to be patient by identifying at least three ways that you can constructively use this time to support your goal.

QUOTES

… Ripening like a tree, which doesn't force its sap, and stands confidently in the storms of spring, not afraid that afterwards summer may not come. It does come. But it comes only to those who are patient, who are there as if eternity lay before them, so unconcernedly silent and vast. I learn it every day of my life, learn it with pain I am grateful for: Patience is everything.

—Rainer Maria Rilke
Persian poet (1828-1910)

The two most powerful warriors are patience and time.

—Leo Tolstoy
Russian author, philosopher (1828-1910)

Patience is not passive; on the contrary, it is active; it is concentrated strength.

—Edward G. Bulwer-Lytton
British Politician, critic, author (1803-1873)

Time accomplishes for the poor what money does for the rich.

—Cesar Chavez
United Farm Workers Labor Union organizer

QUESTIONS AND DEFINITIONS

1. How easy is it for you to be patient with others? How easy is it for you to be patient with yourself?

2. In what way(s) does it serve you to be patient in your life?

3. How does impatience affect your relationships with others?

4. Re-read the Cesar Chavez quote above. How is patience necessary in the application of nonviolent change?

PATIENCE / ACTIVITIES

ACTIVITIES

32.1 Use role-playing to act out some ways in which you are called on everyday, at school and at home, to be patient. Divide the class into groups to develop and present these everyday scenarios where patience is needed for a positive outcome. What helps you to be patient? How does patience relate to nonviolence in these instances?

32.2 Write about a time when someone was patient with you and how that made a difference in your life. What positive qualities empower a person to practice patience? How does their patience empower those around them?

32.3 Write a story showing a hero whose success comes from being patient. Is patience inherent or is it learned in the process? Evaluate and consider alternative points of view involving the portrayed conflict, and other ways in which patience could be expressed by the hero.

DAY 33

APPRECIATION

Louise Hay says, "Praise yourself (and others) as much as you can. The love in our lives begins with us. Loving yourself will help heal this planet." Write down ten things you appreciate about yourself, your so-called enemies, your school, your country, or that you sometimes take for granted.

QUOTES

You have it easily in your power to increase the sum total of this world's happiness now. How? By giving a few words of sincere appreciation to someone who is lonely or discouraged. Perhaps you will forget tomorrow the kind words you say today, but the recipient may cherish them over a lifetime.

—Dale Carnegie
Author, pioneer in the field of building success (1888-1955)

Like when I'm in the bathroom looking at my toilet paper, I'm like "Wow! That's toilet paper!" I don't know if we appreciate how much we have.

—Alicia Silverstone
Actress

Appreciating each other is a true family value, one that will bail out much of the stress on the planet and help strengthen the universal bond all people have.

—Sara Paddison
Author *Hidden Power of the Heart*

There is as much greatness of mind in acknowledging a good turn, as in doing it.

—Seneca
Greek Philosopher, statesman (4 B.C.-65 A.D)

QUESTIONS AND DEFINITIONS

1. What is the one thing that you appreciate most in your life today?

2. What are some acts of appreciation that you have witnessed (i.e., thank you notes, plaques, awards, etc.)? What are some words of appreciation that you like to hear?

3. What are the top three things you appreci-

ate most about yourself, your family, your community, your nation?

4. When was the last time you were publicly praised and how did it feel? Can receiving appreciation make a difference in the kind of work you do?

APPRECIATION / ACTIVITIES

ACTIVITIES

 33.1 Make a journal of appreciation where students can jot down things they appreciate about themselves and those around them. Decorate the pages with pictures and quotes that show appreciation for things, events and people.

 33.2 Write a list of 10 things you appreciate about yourself. Then, make yourself a special award certificate to hang on the wall. Do you behave differently when you feel self-appreciated?

 33.3 Write a short story about someone you know who has made a difference in your life. Let the story serve to appreciate the qualities that make them special. Then write a story about yourself in the third person and do the same thing.

 33.4 Plan an acknowledgment/appreciation dinner for your family. Remember all of the everyday things you do for each other. Notice how far kind words can carry you. Report back to the class.

 33.5 Create a council circle in the classroom. Have students offer three words of praise or appreciation for the person sitting to their left, going clockwise around the circle. The facilitator might choose to set the tone by going first. This activity is meant to explore how simple it is to appreciate something in everyone and to understand how easy it is to help others feel good about themselves. It can also be used as a community building or rebuilding exercise in the resolution of a difficult situation.

 33.6 Make three simple postcards and send a note of appreciation to people in your life who don't ordinarily receive praise for daily, simple tasks well done. (e.g., a cafeteria worker, a bus driver, a mom).

 33.7 Do some local research to discover a hero of peace and justice. What has this person accomplished? How will you appreciate him or her? Create an event or design an award to honor this person's gift to others. Identify the awards that have been established in your community (i.e., Man or Woman of the Year, Local Hero Award, Chamber of Commerce Community Service Recognition, etc.).

DAY 34

LOVE

Gandhi wrote, "Nonviolence is based on the assumption that human nature unfailingly responds to the advances of love." Today, focus on what you appreciate most about the person you like the least.

QUOTES

Love gives meaning, purpose and direction. Doing the work of love, we ensure our survival and our triumph over the forces of evil and destruction.
—bell hooks
> English professor, New York City College; writer,
> philosopher on critical consciousness of self and society

Tell me who you love, and I'll tell you who you are.
—African Proverb

Love takes off the masks that we fear we cannot live without and know we cannot live within.
—James Baldwin
> African American author whose work chronicles the life of the
> American Negro in the 1950s

QUESTIONS AND DEFINITIONS

1. How do you know that you are loved, and how does it make you feel?

2. How do you know when you love someone else? Does it change how you behave?

3. Is it possible to love someone, but not like them? How?

4. What are "acts of love" that you have experienced or witnessed?

5. Some say love is weak; some say love is strong. What is the difference between love that is weak and love that is strong?

6. A key principle of nonviolence is the commitment to oppose the deed, not the doer of the deed. Through the willingness to love, the nonviolent practitioner seeks to open the heart of their adversary. What is meant by "love your enemy?" What is meant by "open the heart" of the adversary? Give examples of how "love" has changed a relationship between individuals or groups of people for the better.

LOVE / ACTIVITIES

ACTIVITIES

 34.1 Have each student bring a jar from home and design his or her own label for a jar of LOVE. Fill it with meaningful trinkets and treasures, or just fill it with thoughts of love. Give it to someone who you think could use some love.

 34.2 Write a short story about enemies who become friends. Make love the central theme in your story.

 34.3 Research what great peacemakers have to say about love and how it has influenced them personally and impacted them as a peacemaker. Write a scene and speak as the peacemaker you select.

 34.4 Do a guided meditation. Have students relax and begin to breathe deeply. Talk them through relaxing the body and the mind. Ask them to imagine a ball of light that is the energy of loving kindness. Let it fill the whole body. Then begin to send it out to the people in your world who you love. Then include the people who aid your daily life from bus driver to crossing guard. Then begin to send it out to your so-called enemies. Discuss your experience after the exercise.

 34.5 Locate and read Dr. Martin Luther King's speech entitled "Loving Your Enemies." Dr. King discusses and defines three kinds of love (romantic love, filial love, and agape love). Have students select one of these three types of love and write a short essay describing themselves as one of these types of love. What do they look like? What can they accomplish? What are their attributes or shortcomings? What have they caused in the world?

 34.6 Write a letter to someone whose love has affected you (living or deceased). Tell them what their support means to you. How has their love made you a better person? (You are not required to send this letter, so feel free to write all of your thoughts.)

DAY 35

UNDERSTANDING

Thich Nhat Hanh says, "When you understand, you cannot help but love. Practice looking at all living beings with the eyes of compassion." Send a silent thought of love to 10 people today. Share your experience with someone.

QUOTE

Peace cannot be kept by force. It can only be achieved by understanding.
—Albert Einstein
Architect of the Theory of Relativity, won the Nobel Prize in physics

QUESTIONS AND DEFINITIONS

1. Describe what it feels like to be understood.

2. What does it mean to "walk in another person's shoes?"

3. When you don't understand someone's motives, how do you feel? How do you act?

4. How does understanding contribute to a more peaceful world?

5. Dialogue about what the difference is between a speaker who is seeking to be understood and one seeking to understand? How does tone of the conversation change depending on the motivation?

ACTIVITIES

 35.1 Use watercolors to paint a picture that describes the feeling tone of understanding. When the page is filled with color, using ink, write a paragraph, over the top of the colored section, about a time when you came to an important understanding. What changed as a result of that understanding? Create a wall of understanding by papering it with these paintings.

 35.2 Write an acrostic poem with the word "understanding." To write an acrostic poem, use each letter of the word "understanding" to begin each new line of the poem.

 35.3 Read some stories from any of the *Chicken Soup for the Soul* books by Jack Canfield and Mark Victor Hansen. After the reading, allow a few moments of silence to reflect on what you feel the story is really about. How does understanding play a part in the story? Debrief.

continued
►

UNDERSTANDING / ACTIVITIES, *continued*

 35.4 Bring to mind someone with whom you don't see eye-to-eye, or an issue about which you have strong feelings. Find a partner and describe the situation or issue. Take the role of your adversary. Now describe the situation from the other point of view. Your partner can role-play being you, or take your position. Role-play for three to five minutes. What was that experience like for you? What did you learn by experiencing the other person's point of view? How might you approach them differently now that you understand them better?

DAY 36

MINDFULNESS

"If we just act in each moment, with composure and mindfulness, each minute of our life is a work of art." Be aware of the motivation behind your action, the intention behind your words and the needs and experiences of other people. By doing so, you are making life more beautiful for yourself and others.

QUOTE

Mindfulness is the practice of doing physical things perfectly, in a state of emptiness in which we become consciously "one" with whatever physical or mental activity we are currently engaged in.

—Master Fwap

Tibetan Buddhist monk, from *Surfing the Himalayas*, by Frederick Lenz

QUESTIONS AND DEFINITIONS

1. Is mindfulness having a full mind? What does it mean to be mindful?
   How is contemplation different from mindfulness?

2. To what daily activities do you bring your complete mindfulness? Name these activities. How does mindfulness change the simplest task?

3. How can mindfulness help prevent and resolve conflict?

ACTIVITIES

 36.1 Choose a simple task, such as eating a strawberry or a handful of blueberries, and bring your complete attention to it. Don't allow yourself to talk to anyone or think of anything else except what you are doing, sensing and feeling. Notice what your hands do, the way the food feels in your mouth, the taste, the texture, the idea of nourishing your body. Is this different from the way you normally eat? How?

36.2 Take the class on a silent walk. Instruct students to pay attention to their surroundings, their feelings, the scents and the colors. Write a paragraph or poem while the sensations and images are still fresh, before beginning to speak or compare notes with classmates. Share these in partners or groups to uncover similarities and differences.

continued ▶

MINDFULNESS / ACTIVITIES, *continued*

36.3 Use a Tibetan bowl or chime to practice mindfulness during a conversation or a group activity such as gardening, walking, rehearsing or teamwork of any kind. When the bell rings, participants agree to stop what they are doing, become silent and make themselves aware of what is going on inside of themselves and around themselves. In other words, pause when the bell rings, then resume the activity or conversation. Did the bell provide you with a heightened sense of what was happening? Did it help you to be more present? Did you enjoy the quiet stillness? Try this practice for a week. What do you notice?

36.4 Interview an athlete or artist about what it is like to be "in the zone." How do different people describe "the zone?" Is there an activity in your life in which you are able to experience this mindfulness, that can put you "in the zone?" How can this practice of mindfulness contribute to your practice of nonviolence? Have a class council circle to reflect on these questions.

DAY 37

GRACIOUSNESS

When you are out today, be more courteous. Give others the right of way, stop and let others pass, hold a door or offer a helping hand.

QUOTE

Deliberate with caution, but act with decision; and yield with graciousness, or oppose with firmness.

—Charles Caleb Colton
Philosopher, statesman (1780-1832)

QUESTIONS AND DEFINITIONS

1. What is graciousness and how does it present itself?

2. What acts of kindness would you consider to be acts of graciousness (e.g., picking up something that another has dropped or helping a teacher with too much to carry)?

3. What are some simple acts of graciousness that you have witnessed or experienced in the last few weeks?

4. How can graciousness contribute to conflict prevention and resolution?

ACTIVITIES

 37.1 Draw recognizable symbols, like road signs, based on simple and everyday acts of graciousness. These can be created on heavy cardboard and laminated to be posted around the classroom, library, lunch area and playground. Design these "gracious" signs to remind others of simple ways in which we can assist in spreading goodwill throughout our community.

37.2 Create skits in class to show the difference between graciousness and selfishness. Show how graciousness promotes inclusivity and enhanced relationships even with total strangers. Show how a host or hostess can be gracious or not.

 37.3 Find at least one opportunity to be gracious daily. Keep a journal for one week and then report back to class. What insights did you have?

DAY 38

KINDNESS

Everyday we hear of random and senseless acts of violence. Participate in the counter-revolution of kindness started by Anne Herbert. Perform three acts of kindness today.

QUOTES

Spread love everywhere you go: first of all, in your own house. Give love to your children, to your wife or husband, to a next door neighbor … Let no one ever come to you without leaving better and happier. Be the living expressions of God's kindness; kindness in your face, kindness in your eyes, kindness in your smile, kindness in your warm greeting.

—Mother Teresa
Humanitarian leader

My religion is simple, my religion is kindness.
— His Holiness, the Dalai Llama
14th spiritual leader of Tibet

If we just worry about the big picture, we are powerless. So my secret is to start right away doing whatever little work I can do. I try to give joy to one person in the morning, and remove the suffering of one person in the afternoon. If you and your friends do not despise the small work, a million people will remove a lot of suffering. That is the secret. Start right now.
— Sister Chän Khöng
Author of *Learning True Love*

QUESTIONS AND DEFINITIONS

1. What are the qualities and behavior of a kind person?

2. What value do we place on "kindness" in our society and how does that affect the world we live in? Explain your answer.

3. Do you think you are a kind person? Why?

4. How could you be more kind in your life? And to whom?

5. How do you think we could teach people to be more kind?

ACTIVITIES

 38.1 Today practice at least three random acts of kindness. Be creative. Make them up as you go along. Seek out opportunities. Then write a short thought paper about your practice. Does a simple act of kindness change the way you feel about yourself or others?

continued ▶

KINDNESS / ACTIVITIES, *continued*

 38.2 Make a class list of acts of kindness that present themselves everyday. See how easy it is and how often you have opportunities to be kind (e.g., to carry groceries, pet a dog, ask how your neighbor is feeling, bring a treat to a teacher or parent.) Cultivate your awareness as a class. Make the list into a beautiful and artistic scroll and display it on campus.

 38.3 Make ribbons or certificates that acknowledge kindness. Make lots of them! Hand them out every time you see someone express kindness today. Keep a list of all the kindnesses. How alert are you? How many ribbons can you give away? Academic awards and prizes only address one aspect of a person. Make the way you treat each other count in your school. Come back and share your experiences. How did people receive the gifts? What was it like to give them away? What was it like to observe so much kindness? What additional opportunities for kindness did you see?

 38.4 Practice kindness in your classroom. Partner students to assist each other in their areas of need.

 38.5 Have the class stand in a large circle and turn to the right. Massage the shoulders of the person in front of you. Then change directions and do it again. How often do you reach out to the others without saying anything? How does it make you feel?

DAY 39

DIALOGUE

Marianne Williamson describes a healthy society as one in which "those who disagree can do so with honor and respect for other people's opinions, and an appreciation for our shared humanity." In the *Desiderata* by Max Ehrmann, he says, "Speak your truth quietly and clearly and listen to others." Today, speak up but do not enter into the spirit of argument.

QUOTES

Dialogue is a conversation on a common subject between two or more persons of differing views. The primary purpose of dialogue is for each person to learn from the other so that he or she can change and grow ... Through this process, we come to a deeper understanding of the issues that both divide and unite us thereby paving the way for cooperation and collaboration.

—Leonard Swidler

Adapted from *Dialogue Decalogue*

Man wishes to be confirmed in his being by man. Secretly, and bashfully, he watches for a "yes," which can come to him only from one human being to another.

—Martin Buber

Theologian, educator, mystic,

expert on dialogue, encounter and community (1878–1965)

Generally speaking, the first nonviolent act is not fasting, but dialogue. The other side, the adversary is recognized as a person, he is taken out of his anonymity and exists in his own right, for what he really is, a person. To engage someone in dialogue is to recognize him, have faith in him. At every step in the nonviolent struggle, at every level we try tirelessly to establish a dialogue, or reestablish it if it has broken down.

—Hildegard Goss-Mayr

Activist, honorary President, Fellowship of Reconciliation

QUESTIONS AND DEFINITIONS

1. What is the difference between debate and dialogue?

2. What does listening have to do with successful dialogue?

3. What is the value in dialogue? How would you feel at the conclusion of a successful dialogue? Does dialogue insist on resolution or agreement?

4. Do you find yourself avoiding conversations with certain people because they more often end in argument than in dialogue? What tools could assist?

DIALOGUE / ACTIVITIES

ACTIVITIES

39.1 Select a controversial topic. Pair up with one other person. Identify yourself as "A" or "B." Speaker A will speak from the pro position on an issue. Speaker B will speak from a con position on the same issue. Try several topics, reversing roles. Present one point of view in the first round of dialogue. Present the opposing view the next time. Share about your paired experiences with the whole class.

39.2 Divide the class into three- or four-person groups and give each group a topic to discuss. Practice allowing each person's talking to be followed by a brief period of silence to reflect on what has been said before the next person speaks. Pay attention to the feelings that come up for you as you listen to others. How successful was your group? Listen with the intention to learn from others. Come back to the whole group and share about the process rather than the topic.

39.3 Have a council circle (as described in *How to Use the Curriculum Guide,* on page xi), on a heated topic on your campus relative to nonviolence. How easy is it to discuss a passionate subject and really listen to other ideas that may not coincide with your own? How easy is it not to have to convince everyone to think like you? Can you listen to other opinions and simply observe the feelings that come up for you? Can you respect other opinions? Select and discuss a current global issue in the same way.

39.4 Speaking through invitation is another way to facilitate group dialogue. One person is asked to begin a discussion. When he or she finishes speaking, that person then invites another participant to share. The second person may speak or decline to speak (choose to pass) and, in turn, invites someone else to speak. Conclude the dialogue after everyone has had the opportunity to speak.

39.5 Another way of facilitating group dialogue is to use a bell or chime. Have everyone agree to stop speaking when it is rung. Seated in a circle, begin an open dialogue on a topic of interest. If the discussion becomes heated, or more than one person is talking at the same time, have the facilitator ring the bell to stop everyone for a moment of silent reflection. How does this change the conversation?

39.6 Work in teams of two or three. Write a dialogue based on a conflict such as a child and parent debating about curfew, a student and teacher debating about a grade, or any other everyday debate or conflict of interest you can think of. In your dialogue, make sure that each character is listening attentively and responding graciously to what the other person is saying. After reading dialogues to the class, debrief based on how realistic these scenes are and why.

continued ▶

DIALOGUE / ACTIVITIES, *continued*

 39.7 Martin Buber is quoted above. Have each student research the educational theories of Martin Buber on "dialogue" and "encounter." Let each one choose a statement that resonates for him or her. In class, have partners exchange statements about "dialogue." Debrief as a class. What did you learn about dialogue? What did you learn about your partner?

DAY 40

UNITY

Differences give variety to life and are often only revealed on the surface anyway. Today, look for three ways to see beyond outer differences in opinions, appearances or goals. Find the meeting point of underlying unity that exists in diversity.

QUOTES

Behold how good and how pleasant it is for brethren to dwell together in unity.

—Holy Bible
Book of Psalms 133

By standing together in unity, solidarity and love, we will heal the wounds in the earth and in each other. We can make a positive difference through our actions.

—Julia Butterfly Hill
Activist, ecologist

We are not going to be able to operate our Spaceship Earth successfully nor for much longer unless we see it as a whole spaceship and our fate as common. It has to be everybody or nobody.

—Buckminster Fuller
Author, engineer, mathematician, architect (1895-1983)

Solidarity is not a matter of sentiment but a fact, cold and impassive as the granite foundations of a skyscraper. If the basic elements, identity of interest, clarity of vision, honesty of intent, and oneness of purpose, or any of these is lacking, all sentimental pleas for solidarity, and all efforts to achieve it will be barren of results.

—Noam Chomsky
Professor of linguistics at MIT, author, educator, astute critic of U.S. foreign policy

QUESTIONS AND DEFINITIONS

1. What unifies us and what separates us?

2. What does "unity in diversity" mean?

3. What are the things that you have in common with the whole class? What things are different? How can you be different and still have unity?

UNITY / ACTIVITIES

ACTIVITIES

 40.1 Make a unity chain. Have each student in the whole school decorate a strip of paper. Then create an assembly/ceremony to make one magnificent chain out of all the links. How is the whole greater than the sum of its parts?

 40.2 Write a poem on unity and nonviolence. Each member of the class writes a line or two and sees only the line immediately above his starting point. Have several people read the same poem and enjoy several interpretations of the lines.

 40.3 Create a collage, unity quilt or mobile. Each piece could represent each individual in the class or it could represent their vision of peace. Put the individual pieces together to share the vision of the whole class.

DAY 41

OPENNESS

A Turkish proverb says, "He who builds himself a fence, fences out more than he fences in." Today, be open to understanding ideas and people that you have previously excluded.

QUOTES

Let go of your attachment to being right, and suddenly your mind is more open. You're able to benefit from the unique viewpoints of others, without being crippled by your own judgment.

—**Ralph Marston**
South Australian author, biochemist (1900-1965)

We hate some persons because we do not know them; and we will not know them because we hate them.

—**Charles Caleb Colton**
Philosopher, statesman (1780-1832)

QUESTIONS AND DEFINITIONS

1. What are different ways of responding to something or someone new and different?

2. How do little children respond to new experiences, objects, people, situations?

3. What are the advantages and risks of being open to new people? New ideas?

4. In what ways do you consider yourself to be an open-minded person in conversation, making new friends, or selecting teams, etc.?

5. Think of at least one stereotype, judgment or belief that you hold about a group of people. How does your stereotype serve you? What would it take for you to be open to a new idea, or a new experience of that group? If you were to let go of your stereotypes, how would that change you? Your world?

6. Relative to nonviolence, about what ideas would you like to be more open-minded?

7. How do you balance openness and staying safe in new situations?

ACTIVITIES

41.1 At lunch time go beyond your comfort zone and introduce yourself to someone to whom you have never spoken. What happened? What did you find out about yourself and about the other person?

continued ▶

OPENNESS / ACTIVITIES, *continued*

 41.2 Find a partner in class whom you don't know very well and interview him or her. Ask the following questions: In what do you believe? Who loves you? How do you know? What do you hate? What do you love? What is something that most people don't know about you? Is it easy or more difficult to speak about your deep feelings with someone who doesn't know you very well?

 41.3 Identify a situation such as the first day of school, moving to a new neighborhood, choosing teams or looking for a seat in the cafeteria. On a blank sheet of paper, draw yourself in this situation with thought bubbles all around your head. What thoughts are going through your mind as you approach the situation? When the drawings are complete, debrief the activity by assessing which thoughts demonstrate your judgmental nature and which thoughts demonstrate your openness. Can awareness of your own thoughts help you to become more open in these situations?

 41.4 Write a narrative about your life while pretending to be someone else who is very different from yourself. When you have completed your paper, read it out loud in class or to a partner. Answer the following questions on the back of your paper before turning it in: What happens when you shift your perspective and view the world through someone else's eyes? Does it help to break down stereotypes? Has this exercise helped you to be more open to others?

 41.5 Identify a topic about which class members have strong feelings, pro and con. Find partners with different points of view. Designate a speaker and a listener. The listener begins by saying, "I am open to listening to your point of view. I am open to understanding your point of view. I invite you to share your thoughts and feelings with me."

The speaker then has three minutes to share their point of view and why they see things that way.

When the speaker finishes sharing, the listener responds, "Thank you for sharing with me." Then the listener shares what they heard the speaker say and at least one thing they heard that helps them understand the speaker's point of view. When you understand, you don't have to agree; you just understand.

When both parties are complete, share your experiences in a large group.

DAY 42

ACCOUNTABILITY

In conflicting situations, personal accountability allows us to take responsibility for how we contribute to the conflict. Today, take responsibility for how you contribute to a conflict and make a different choice that can lead to a peaceful resolution.

QUOTE

It is not only what we do, but also what we do not do, for which we are accountable.
—**Moliere**
French playwright in the court of Louis IVX (1622-1672)

QUESTIONS AND DEFINITIONS

1. In what areas of your life are you accountable for your own actions and agreements? In what areas are your parents still accountable for your behavior?

2. How often are your decisions based on personal accountability? How often are they based on not wanting to be caught or punished? What is the difference?

3. How can you be accountable without accepting blame? What is the difference?

4. How does being accountable for your choices and actions contribute to a better community?

ACTIVITIES

42.1 Be accountable for your words. Today, make a list of every thought you think and every word you speak that is violent (e.g., judgmental, critical, unkind, diminishing). Every time that you become aware, neutralize what you have said, by repeating to yourself: "Cancel, erase, delete."

42.2 Next, replace the violent thought or word with words that are healing. Write down the healing words opposite the violent ones. What did you learn about yourself? What did you learn about being accountable? Notice that only when you become accountable, are you able to take charge and make a change.

42.3 Create and portray several scenarios where one might respond with blame or denial. Role-play alternative actions and choices based on personal accountability. Include personal experiences or an incident reported in the news.

continued ▶

ACCOUNTABILITY / ACTIVITIES, *continued*

 42.4 We sometimes forget that we are accountable for what we don't do as well as what we do. If a citizen does not vote, he is still accountable for who gets elected. Why? If you see someone in trouble and do not take action, to some degree you are accountable for what happened.

Think of a situation in which you did not speak or did not act and how you are accountable for the outcome in that situation. Write about it. Remember to practice self-forgiveness. What did you learn from this experience?

 42.5 Tell a story, write an essay or act out a scenario in which you were asked to do something that was against your better judgment. Choose to be accountable for what happened. What did you do? Why? What were the consequences?

DAY 43

UNIQUENESS

Hazrat Inyayat Khan says, "Each human personality is like a piece of music, having an individual tone and rhythm of its own." Today, let the music of who you are, play. Also, look for the unique qualities and talents of those around you, whom you may sometimes take for granted.

QUOTES

There is a vitality, a life force, an energy, a quickening that is translated through you into action and because there is only one of you in all time, this expression is unique, and if you block it, it will never exist through any other medium and be lost. The world will not have it.

—Martha Graham
Pioneer of Modern Dance & Expressionism (1894-1991)

When will we teach our children what they are? One should say to each of them: Do you know what you are? You are a marvel! You are unique! In all the world, there is no other child exactly like you! In the millions of years that have passed, there has never been another child like you! ... You have the capacity for anything! Yes, you are a marvel, and when you grow up, can you harm another who is like you, a marvel?

—Pablo Casals
Conductor, cellist, artist (1876-1973)

QUESTIONS AND DEFINITIONS

1. How are you unique? What makes you unique?

2. How do you appreciate and express your uniqueness?

3. What is unique about your family, your school and your community?

4. How are we all enriched by the uniqueness of others? How does one's uniqueness relate to the practice of nonviolence?

5. Knowing that we are all unique, how easy or difficult is it to share your ideas and gifts with your peers, your parents and your teachers? How can you create a space for others to express their uniqueness?

ACTIVITIES

 43.1 Each student is given a "personal apple." They are to consider it closely and write at least 20 adjectives that describe that particular apple. If there is time, the facilitator may ask the students to write a short paragraph from the point of view of the apple. They may not mark or eat the apple! When the writing is complete, the teacher collects all the apples and puts them together in a box. The students then attempt to distinguish their "personal apple" by what they wrote. Another fruit, or a rock may be substituted.

continued ▶

UNIQUENESS / ACTIVITIES, *continued*

 43.2 Draw, write, dance or create a free art project about the ways in which you are unique and special. Let your project express your uniqueness.

 43.3 Bring a symbol of your uniqueness to class. Write a title and gallery comment for your item on a 3x5 card. Then place the symbols around the classroom and take a gallery walk. You may want to share the symbols out loud as the exhibit is taking place or you may want to have the class view in silence and write a review after the exhibit.

 43.4 Collect stories from your parents and grandparents about your family's history, good times and challenges, and collect small items and pictures that symbolize these events. Create a Memory Box art project with these things (e.g., a fish hook to represent a family fishing trip).

DAY 44

COOPERATION

When we work together, we are stronger than when we work alone. Today, find one significant way that you can cooperate more effectively with the people in your family or workplace, school or community. Do it.

QUOTES

...We know that our happiness will not come from the goods we have, but from the good we do together.

—John Fitzgerald Kennedy

35th President of the U.S., champion of Civil Rights, respected as leader of the Free World (1917-1963)

Every kind of peaceful cooperation among men is primarily based on mutual trust and only secondarily on institutions such as courts of justice and police.

—Albert Einstein

Author of the *Theory of Relativity* (1879-1955)

People who work together will win, whether it is against complex football defenses, or the problems of modern society.

—Vince Lombardi

Green Bay Packer's Coach, five time football Hall of Famer

When we truly cooperate, it is possible to hear an ensemble voice and catch a group vision, which speaks louder and more inclusively than any individual voice or vision.

—Peggy Dobreer

Writer, educator, co-Author of *64 Ways to Practice Nonviolence*

It is through cooperation, rather than conflict, that your greatest successes will be derived.

—Ralph Charell

English author

QUESTIONS AND DEFINITIONS

1. Compare and contrast working competitively with working cooperatively.

2. What does cooperation have to do with non-violence?

3. When was the last time you did a cooperative project? Were there any challenges that the group faced? Identify them.

4. In what ways has cooperative work been challenging for you in the past? What might you have to relinquish in order to more effectively cooperate?

COOPERATION / ACTIVITIES

ACTIVITIES

 44.1 Have all the students sit on the floor (arm's distance apart) in a designated area of a classroom or field. The task is to keep a balloon up in the air as long as possible, while remaining seated at all times during the exercise. Try a couple of times and debrief in terms of what worked and what did not? Then try again. What did the class learn about working together?

 44.2 Create a classroom symbol of cooperation as a cooperative project. Decide as a group how your classroom will work together as a team and what you would like to create.

 44.3 Make a pot of soup together as a class. Make a list of who will bring what and about what each person will be responsible for: shopping, chopping, stirring, serving, cleaning, etc. Read the story *Stone Soup* while you are enjoying your Cooperative Soup together.

 44.4 Try to pick up a heavy table by yourself. How easy is it with six or seven people helping? Does brawn weigh as heavily as cooperation in this task?

 44.5 Have the entire group line up at one end of the room with ankles touching on both sides. The challenge is to get to the other side of the room without loosing contact at any point. You may not tie ankles together. Each time any two ankles loose contact, the entire group must start over. Preset a specific amount of time that you will play (15 minutes is suggested). Debrief in terms of cooperative effort and the emergence of leadership.

 44.6 Steven Covey says that "the challenge is to apply the principles of creative cooperation which we learn from nature, in our social interactions." With what forms of cooperation in nature are you familiar? What does nature have to teach us about cooperation?

 44.7 Explore examples of groups and communities who have cooperated to create nonviolent change. What did they have to "give up" in order to cooperate? What did they have to "call forward from within" themselves or the group? Examples include: Sarvodaya Movement in Sri Lanka, Sanctuary Movement in the U.S. (1980's), Freedom Summer in Mississippi (1964), Le Chambon Sur Lignon in France (1940), city of Billings, Montana (Not in Our Town Campaign), Community of Peace People in Ireland (1970's). Present your findings to the class.

DAY 45

MASTERY

Labor organizer Cesar Chavez teaches, "If you use violence, you have to sell part of yourself for that violence. Then you are no longer a master of your own struggle." Breathe deeply, silently counting backwards from 10 to calm yourself and cool off before you speak or act with impatience or anger. Do this at least once today.

QUOTES

One can have no smaller or greater mastery than mastery of oneself.
—Leonardo de Vinci
Philosopher, painter, pioneer of the Italian Renaissance (1452-1519)

Personal mastery teaches us to choose. Choosing is a courageous act: picking the results and actions, which you will make into your destiny.
—Peter Senge
Educator, author

Throwing down your sword is also an art of war. If you have attained mastery of swordlessness, you will never be without a sword. The opponent's sword is your sword.
—Yagyu Munenori
Author of *Family Traditions on the Art of War*

We decide our own fate by our actions. You have to gain mastery over your self …
It is not a matter of sitting back and accepting
—Aung San Suu Kyi
Human Rights activist, leader of pro-democracy movement in Burma

QUESTIONS AND DEFINITIONS

1. What does it mean "to master something?" What does it mean to have mastery over yourself?

2. Give examples of people who are accomplished in their field. What have they had to master in order to be great?

3. What have you mastered in your life (physical, mental and emotional skills)?

4. How do skills, habits, intention, discipline, compassion and feedback relate to mastery?

5. What are you working to master? How will you know you have achieved mastery?

6. Explore the relationship between the mind, emotions and actions in the development of mastery.

MASTERY / ACTIVITIES

ACTIVITIES

45.1 "Master the Feeling"—Use the breathing practice above to calm yourself before acting in a destructive way. Breathe in and out while counting backwards.

45.2 Write about something you would like to master in your life. Make a list of steps that you must take in order to accomplish it. Include vision, skills, actions, resources and needs. How will you know when you have achieved mastery and what will be the measurement or gift of the journey? See and draw yourself in that masterful state. Include it in your project as a cover illustration.

45.3 Read the following excerpt that Cesar Chavez wrote in his Letter from Delano:

"Our strikers here in Delano and those who represent us throughout the world are well trained for this struggle. They have been under the gun, they have been kicked and beaten and herded by dogs, they have been cursed and ridiculed, they have been stripped and chained and jailed, they have been sprayed with the poisons used in the vineyards; but they have been taught not to lie down and die nor to flee in shame, but to resist with every ounce of human endurance and spirit. To resist, not with retaliation in kind, but to overcome, with love and compassion and patient tenacity, with truth and public appeal, with friends and allies, with nobility and discipline, with politics and law, and with prayer and fasting. They were not trained in a month or even a year; after all, this new harvest season will mark our fourth full year of strike and even now we continue to plan and prepare for the years to come."

Discuss the letter in terms of the kind of mastery that was required from the strikers in Delano. What does it teach you about "soul force?" How disciplined did the strikers have to be? Could you have endured as they did for something you believed in? Write a speech as one of those Delano strikers to describe what it took to endure or write one as your self to describe some kind of mastery you have employed in some area of your life that you believe in. What was your goal? What did you encounter?
(from *The Universe Bends Toward Justice: A Reader on Christian Nonviolence in the U.S.*, edited by Angie O'Gorman, Philadelphia, New Society Publishing)

45.4 What must a practitioner of nonviolence master in himself? What would you like to master in your practice of nonviolence? Write about someone who has mastered this. How did they do it? What difference will it make in your life as you master this skill? Develop a plan for developing mastery in this area; include small, specific steps that you can practice over the next 30 days. Write about the process you are willing to go through. Create a project that shares your results.

45.5 How did student activists during the Civil Rights Movement develop the self-mastery to practice nonviolence during sit-ins, demonstrations and freedom rides? Learn about Rev. James Lawson, Jr., the Civil Rights Movement's architect of nonviolence. See *A Force More Powerful* or read *Freedom Song* or *The Children* (See Video Resource Guide). Write a thought paper that describes these practices and skills. Could you master them? How are they applied today?

DAY 46

COMPASSION

Mother Teresa implored us to "find someone who thinks he is alone and let him know that he is not." Today, do as Mother Teresa suggests.

QUOTES

It's not how much we give, but how much love we put in the doing—that's compassion in action.
—Mother Teresa
Albanian nun, 1979 Nobel Peace Prize Recipient (1910-1997)

Compassion is the basis of morality.
—Arnold Schopenhauer
Early 19th century German philosopher

Until he extends his circle of compassion to include all living things, man will not himself find peace.
—Albert Schweitzer
Humanitarian, physician (1865-1937)

QUESTIONS AND DEFINITIONS

Compassion:
  (Latin) "... to feel with ... identify with."
  (Hebrew) "... feeling that comes from the depth (womb or bowels) of Life."

1. How does compassion differ from sympathy? When was the last time you witnessed an expression of compassion?

2. What is the distinction between compassion as a feeling versus compassion as a practice?

3. Some people are naturally compassionate. Do you think others can learn it?

4. If you are compassionate, how do you know it and when did you first discover it?

5. What is required of you in order to experience compassion for yourself? For others?

6. Can you be compassionate and angry, hurt and upset at the same time? Explain your response.

7. How does the principle of compassion fit into the practice of nonviolence? A culture of nonviolence?

COMPASSION / ACTIVITIES

ACTIVITIES

46.1 Use watercolors to create a painting that describes compassion. Then use poetry or prose to describe your watercolor.

46.2 Write an acrostic poem of the word "compassion." An acrostic poem uses each letter in a word as the first letter of each line in a poem about that word.

46.3 Study the life of Mother Teresa as an example of compassion in action. What acts will you perform weekly similar to hers? Chart your weekly experiences based on the type of act and the number of positive responses.

46.4 What opportunity do you have to practice compassion today? Be specific. Do it. Break into small groups and share your experience or write about your experience in your journal. What did you do? How did it affect the other person? How did it impact you? What did you learn?

46.5 Write a short story about how an act of compassion made a difference (e.g., in your family, in another country, in your neighborhood, in history, between generations, between enemies, between children and parents).

46.6 Write a short thought paper to compare and contrast one of the following pairs of words and concepts: compassion and charity, compassion and sympathy, compassion and pity, compassion and blame, or compassionate thought and compassionate action. Begin by defining the pair you chose. As your essay develops, consider the comparison in terms of your understanding of nonviolence.

COMMUNITY

Nonviolence challenges us to stand for truth

by taking action that honors the dignity and worth

of every human being.

DAY 47

DISARMAMENT

Have a conversation with someone today about what the world would be like if there were no weapons nor any need for them. Imagine such a world.

QUOTES

Someday, the demand for disarmament, by hundreds of millions will, I hope, become so universal and so insistent that no man, no nation, can withstand it.

—General Dwight Eisenhower

34th U.S. president, commander of Armed Forces in WWII

You cannot serve two masters. You cannot prepare for war and expect to have peace.

—Albert Einstein

Winner of the Nobel Prize in Physics, advocate for nuclear disarmament

QUESTIONS AND DEFINITIONS

1. List different kinds of disarmament. Discuss and rate them in order of importance to you and to the class.

2. What is a handgun for? What is a rifle for? What is an automatic weapon for? What are nuclear weapons for? How do weapons impact your life, your community, our nation, the world?

3. How do you feel about owning a gun and using it? Why?

4. What do you think about the ownership and use of nuclear weapons?

5. How would disarmament change our world?

6. What do you think about the international proliferation and use of nuclear weapons? How might nuclear disarmament affect a country?

ACTIVITIES

 47.1 Have a poster art show depicting disarmament and life without weapons. Ask the class to decide how these posters could be of value and with whom they would like to share them. Create an exhibit of poster art depicting life with and without weapons. Posters might be about choice, vision, what weapons cost us, alternatives to weapons, or other related ideas. Let the class decide on how these posters could be of value and where they should hang.

continued ▶

DISARMAMENT/ ACTIVITIES, *continued*

 47.2 Invite students to share personal stories of how gun violence has affected them (personal experiences, news, entertainment). They may use prose/poetry/art/theatre. They may work in groups or solo as preferred. Teacher should suggest a balance for presentations to students, parents, community. You may want to use school newspapers, public presentations, bulletin boards or art shows to share results.

 47.3 Invite local organizations that provide speakers to talk about consequences of gun violence (parents who have lost children to gun violence, youths who are victims of gun violence) to speak to your group. Ask your local police department, Mothers Against Gun Violence, etc. for referrals. What can be done?

 47.4 Research how other countries function without public gun ownership (e.g., Great Britain, Holland, Japan, etc.). Compare and contrast two of these countries in outline form and write a brief summary of what you learned. What will disarmament mean in your school? What will people disarm themselves of? How will they disarm? What will you do with the arms? How will you celebrate?

 47.5 Develop and implement a disarmament campaign at your school.

 47.6 How has access to guns affected the experience of being a student today? Interview other individuals on campus for opinions and stories. Develop a questionnaire and create a graph to record statistics regarding the differing views of administrators, students, teachers and employees.

 47.7 Compare and contrast national disarmament versus personal disarmament. What are the pros and cons of each? Facilitate research on this topic and organize a class debate.

 47.8 Research the role of weapons sales within the U.S. national economy and international economies. How much does the sale of weapons impact our economy? To whom do we sell weapons? Have a debate about arms sales.

 47.9 Princess Diana of Wales was involved in a particular type of disarmament program. Use the Internet or other sources to learn about her visits to other countries regarding this issue. Find out who received a Nobel Peace Prize for her work in this same area of disarmament. Research statistics about the scope of this problem throughout the world, the U.S. position on this issue, and names of three organizations that are involved with this problem. What are your thoughts on this issue?

continued ▶

DISARMAMENT / ACTIVITIES, *continued*

 47.10 Choose a country that participates in nuclear armament. Find out how much nuclear weapons cost each year in that country. Consider storage, research and development, manufacture, deployment, and clean up. Research the particular needs of the country and the ways in which that money might otherwise be spent. After completing and presenting this research, allow the class to hold a council dialogue to consider the efficacy and use of nuclear weapons.

 47.11 Research and write about the effects of the nuclear weapons on the people of Hiroshima. Who were the Hiroshima Maidens? Imagine what it would be like to walk in a Hiroshima Maiden's shoes. Write and deliver a comment to the people of America while assuming the character of a Hiroshima Maiden.

DAY 48

ECOLOGY

Value the earth by conserving natural resources and avoiding the purchase of products that deplete rain forests or exploit labor forces. Practice recycling today by using at least one recycled product or by recycling a product.

QUOTES

We have a special responsibility to the ecosystem of this planet. In making sure that other species survive, we will be nurturing the survival of our own.

—Dr. Wangari Maathai

Nobel Peace Laureate and founder of the Green Belt Movement

Only after the last tree has been cut down, only after the last river has been poisoned, only after the last fish has been caught, only then will you find that money cannot be eaten.

—Cree Indian Prophecy

Largest, most important tribe north of Mexico

Pollution is nothing but resources we're not using.

—Buckminster Fuller

Mathematician, engineer, architect, author (1895-1983)

Everything is connected to everything else. Everything must go somewhere. Nature knows best. There is no such thing as a free lunch. If you don't put something in the ecology, it's not there.

—Barry Commoner

Author of *Five Laws of Ecology*, environmentalist

QUESTIONS AND DEFINITIONS

1. Research and conduct an assessment of your home or school. How environmentally safe and environmentally friendly are they?

2. What are the ways that you and your family support the ecology of the planet?

3. What are ways in which your community either supports or destroys the ecology in your area?

4. What does "sustainability" mean?

5. Discuss the ecology of your own body. What things do you do to support and protect your personal environment?

E C O L O G Y / ACTIVITIES

ACTIVITIES

Visit www.earthday.org and www.coopamerica.org

48.1 Plan and implement a class ecology project. Examples: Start a recycling program at school, grow an organic garden, plant a tree, have an eco-education day, bring younger students to a local nature area, etc.

48.2 Adopt a beach, wetlands, forest, or other natural environment. Have a field trip and spend the day exploring, cleaning, restoring and enjoying it. Individually or collectively, commit to consciously caring for this precious environment throughout the year.

48.3 Use the Internet or library to learn about Kenya's Greenbelt Movement, the Chipko Tree Hugger Movement, Earth Day, the Goldman Environmental Prize, the Uwa Indians of Columbia, Dr. Vandana Shiva of India. How did they apply nonviolent strategies toward environmental balance? Divide the class into groups of four or five students for each topic. Have each group present its findings to the class.

48.4 Research companies and organizations that are helping the environment today. (Check with your Chamber of Commerce or local environmental organizations.) Find one that chooses sustainability as a priority. Plan a field trip for a tour of this business and interview policy makers.

48.5 Identify an environmental cause that you would like to support. Create an educational program and fundraiser to support their activities.

DAY 49

HONOR

Albert Einstein said, "There are only two ways to live your life. One is as though nothing is a miracle. The other is as if everything is." Before each meal today, stop to honor all the hands that brought it to you and to bless the earth for its bounty.

QUOTES

A man has honor if he holds himself to an ideal of conduct though it is inconvenient, unprofitable, or dangerous to do so.
> **—Walter Lippman**
> American author and journalist (1889-1974)

When there is lack of honor in the government, the morals of the whole people are poisoned.
> **—Herbert Hoover**
> 31st U.S. president, humanitarian (1874-1964)

Dignity does not consist in possessing honors, but in deserving them.
> **—Aristotle**
> Greek philosopher and statesman (384-322 B.C)

No amount of ability is of the slightest avail without honor.
> **—Thomas Carlyle**
> Scottish author, essayist, historian (1795-1881)

QUESTIONS AND DEFINITIONS

1. What does if feel like to be truly honored? What do people say to honor you? How do they act?

2. What are the ways in which you honor the people and traditions in your life?

3. How do you honor yourself?

4. What are the things our culture honors with which you do not agree? With what things do you agree?

5. How do different cultures show "honor" to one another?

ACTIVITIES

49.1 Create a five-minute project to honor the best things about you. Present it to the class. You may use art, music, theater, words, pictures or anything else that expresses your best self in community.

continued ▶

HONOR/ ACTIVITIES, *continued*

 49.2 Make a vocabulary list of honorable traits and people in history or in your family who carry these traits. It is good to reflect on who our role models are and why. Make a mobile of honorable traits or a family tree of the your honorable family members and their traits.

 49.3 Do a class cooking project. Honor each ingredient; how it was grown and who tended to it. Hold good thoughts for your lives, which are nourished by the food you eat together. Write a poem or meal blessing.

 49.4 Honor those people at school who serve you on a daily basis. Create title and honorary degrees as an art project and give them out in a special assembly to let the people around you know that you honor their contribution to your life no matter how large or small.

 49.5 Honor yourself, your school and those around you for working the *64 Ways*. Write songs, create awards, begin to organize the Day 64 Celebration you will have with your class or community in two weeks' time. See page 163.

49.6 What traditions in your family or culture honor ancestors? Reflect on your ancestors—your family, your ethnicity, your nationality, etc. What sacrifices did they make, what courageous actions did they take so you could be here? What were their finest qualities and contributions? Honor your ancestors through poetry, song or drama in a class presentation.

DAY 50

CHOICE

Be aware today of any jokes or remarks that show disrespect toward ethnic groups, women or men, classes of people, religious groups, gays or lesbians. Be considerate of every person's dignity, and choose not to participate in disrespectful conversation.

QUOTES

We are not permitted to choose the frame of our destiny. But what we put into it is ours.
—Dag Hammarskjöld
Swedish diplomat, Secretarial General of the United Nations, posthumously received the Nobel Peace Prize (1905-1961)

Every person is an activist, whether we realize it or not, because every choice we make changes the world. It is up to us to decide to be activists for healing or for suffering, for creating or destroying.
—Julia Butterfly Hill
Environmentalist

The artist must elect to fight for freedom or slavery. I have made my choice. I had no alternative.
—Paul Robeson
Artist, activist

QUESTIONS AND DEFINITIONS

1. Nonviolent choices affirm life; they are pro-people. Violent choices are anti-people; they hurt or diminish life. Give examples of each in your personal life, relationships, community, school.

2. What does it take to make choices that may not coincide with those around you?

3. Share a difficult choice you had to make. How did you make your decision? What did you feel when you made it? What were the consequences of your choice?

4. What choices have you made regarding violence in your life? Nonviolence? Think of a time that you participated in violence (in thought, word or deed). What determined your choice? What other choices were possible?

5. When a person chooses nonviolence, what are they choosing to let go of? What are they choosing to embrace?

CHOICE / ACTIVITIES

ACTIVITIES

50.1 Learn about heroes of nonviolence and the difficult choices they made for peace: Muhammad Ali, Dietrich Bonhoeffer, Eugene Debs. Aung San Suu Kyi, Lech Walesa, Fannie Lou Hamer, Children of the Columbian Peace Movement, Paul Robeson, Harriet Tubman, Ann Bigelow, Alice Paul. Write a letter that your hero might have written about the cause for which they stood. Let the letter clarify the choices they made for peace and why.

50.2 "We always have a choice." Ask students to write about what comes up for them when they hear this. Ask if they ever feel as if they don't have a choice. In those situations, what is lacking or what do they need? Write a thought paper, rap or poem on choice.

50.3 Divide the class into groups of four or five. Develop and write scenes that call for a choice between violence and nonviolence. Role-play these scenes. Let the characters present the pros and cons of the choices. What are obstacles to a peaceful solution? What are available options? What do the characters choose?

50.4 In the midst of his experience in the death camps of Germany, and after his whole family perished in the gas chambers, Victor Frankel discovered what he later called "the last of the human freedoms," ... the ability to "choose one's attitude in any given set of circumstances" (excerpted from *Man's Search for Meaning*).

Facilitate a class dialogue about the power of choice in determining how we experience life. How can we become more aware in making choices? What resources do we have (e.g., imagination, will, self-mastery, etc.)?

DAY 51

ADVOCACY

"When someone stands up to violence," says Thich Nhat Hanh, "a force for change is released. Every action for peace requires someone to exhibit the courage to challenge violence and inspire love." Today be an ally. Without blaming or judging others, speak out for those who are disrespected.

QUOTES

I saw within my own actions a chance to be either a part of the problem or part of the solution.

—Julia Butterfly Hill
Tree sitting activist (1974–)

They came first for the Communists, and I didn't speak up because I wasn't a Communist.

Then they came for the Jews, and I didn't speak up because I wasn't a Jew.

Then they came for the trade unionists, and I didn't speak up because I wasn't a trade unionist.

Then they came for the Catholics, but I didn't speak up because I was a Protestant.

Then they came for me, and by that time no one was left to speak up.

—Pastor Martin Niemoeller
German minister who resisted the Third Reich

QUESTIONS AND DEFINITIONS

1. What is advocacy?

2. Who are your advocates? Describe how they advocate for you.

3. Why is it important to advocate for what you believe?

4. Have you ever been in a difficult situation and felt as though no one was on your side? What happened? How would an advocate have made a difference to you?

ACTIVITIES

 51.1 Recount a time when an advocate came forward and changed the outcome on your behalf. Write a short story and illustrate it.

continued ▶

ADVOCACY / **ACTIVITIES,** *continued*

 51.2 What is required to be an effective advocate? Identify an issue that the group feels strongly about. To whom will you advocate? Develop a school wide campaign to advocate regarding this issue. Make a plan. Implement. Organize. Evaluate.

 51.3 Contact a local newspaper or TV station and let them know what your school is doing to promote nonviolence on campus. Have each student write an article. Read them in class. Then have the class select, and list on the board, the elements from all the articles that they believe will be most effective to communicate to others. Send one article written cooperatively from the class to the newspaper or TV station.

 51.4 Contact an advocacy group that supports the philosophy of the class as a whole and participate in supporting that group as volunteers, with fundraising or by writing letters to your elected officials.

 51.5 Learn about advocacy in your own community. Attend a public meeting or town hall. What issues are being addressed? Who initiated the action? What is being requested of the attendees? Write about your feelings and what you learned from the people who spoke.

 51.6 Research youth-generated advocacy in your community or the world. Learn what other young people have done to advocate for important issues in their countries or communities. Issues might include youth justice, human rights, HIV/AIDS activism, sober living, child labor, education, poverty, environmental justice, peace and justice. Contact the following youth advocacy resources: www.freechild.org, www.youthactivism.com, www.globalyouthactionnetwork.youthparliament. Have students present research to the class.

 51.7 Organize a panel of youth leaders from your own community. Ask them to speak about what they have done and why they did it. What qualities did these youth leaders demonstrate? Write a response to the panel. Explore the power of young people in making a better world.

DAY 52

EQUALITY

Have you ever noticed the groups of people who are under-represented in your activities and lifestyle? Find one way to connect with a person from these groups today.

QUOTE

We hold these truths to be self-evident; that all men are created equal; that they are endowed, by their Creator with certain inalienable rights; that among these are life, liberty, and the pursuit of happiness.

—**United States Declaration of Independence**

QUESTIONS AND DEFINITIONS

1. Is it true, as our Constitution states, that all men are created equal? In what areas of our society do we fall short of honoring and supporting this pledge? Why? In what ways do we honor this pledge?

2. Does being equal mean being the same?

3. Do you think students are treated with equality at school? Explain your answer.

4. What is the meaning of equal access? Equal opportunity? Equal resources?

ACTIVITIES

 52.1 Watch a film on the Civil Rights movement and write a thought paper on your response. Other films might address themes of equal/unequal treatment for women, different ethnicities, immigrants, religious groups, gay and lesbian people, youth. See the video, *Free at Last* from Teaching Tolerance.

 52.2 Read newspapers and periodicals for articles addressing the struggle for equality among groups in society. What do you think should be done to address this situation?

 52.3 Learn more about the Blue-eyed/Brown-eyed experiment created by Jane Elliot, a powerful experiential teaching tool about prejudice, stereotyping, oppression, tyranny and internalized oppression. *(Video available through Facing History and Ourselves. See program resources.)*

continued ▶

EQUALITY / ACTIVITIES, *continued*

 52.4 Read the *Scapegoat Generation* by Mike Males. Or, the facilitator can select excerpts from this text and use them to explore prejudice against youth in our society. How do myths and stereotypes promote inequality in our society? Write a thought paper.

 52.5 Invite the class to research and debate affirmative action. Why do some people oppose it while others support it so passionately? Support your position with facts in a paper. Use this as an opportunity to explore the concept of institutional violence (See *64 Ways* Curriculum, page 10).

 52.6 What kind of people don't you see in your immediate community? With whom don't you come in contact (i.e., which groups of people: people of different religions, immigrants vs. non-immigrants, heterosexuals vs. homosexuals, etc.)? Plan an event in which you can meet and mingle with other communities. Discuss the differences between tolerance, acceptance and inclusivity.

 52.7 Invite a human relations organization to facilitate a dialogue between your group and another group you would like to know. Plan to have a pot luck meal together with ice breakers, dialogue, or games designed to facilitate communication and interaction among different groups. What did you learn?

52.8 Compare and contrast how inequality (i.e. prejudice and discrimination) hurts and/or empowers both the privileged group and the disadvantaged group. Give examples. Research three examples in nonviolence history (research can include film, websites, visits to organizations, exhibits, and/or interviews).

DAY 53

ACTION

"Each of us can work to change a small portion of events and in the total of all those acts will be written the history of this generation," said Robert Kennedy. Today, find a way to make one small change that will contribute to the well-being of your home, school, workplace or community.

QUOTES

My actions are my only true belongings. I cannot escape the consequences of my actions. My actions are the ground on which I stand.
> **—Thich Nhat Hanh**
> Vietnamese Buddhist monk, peace activist

Nobody made a greater mistake than he who did nothing because he could only do a little.
> **—Edmund Burke**
> British statesman, orator, political philosopher (1729-1797)

Washing one's hands of the conflict between the powerful and the powerless means to side with the powerful, not to be neutral.
> **—Paulo Friere**
> International educator, author, activist, theorist

The heart of the matter now is not what governments should do, but what the rest of us must do to turn our governments, and the other organizations that turn to violence to achieve their ends, to the path of peace.
> **—Andrew Lichterman**
> Program Director of Western States Legal Foundation and
> **John Burroughs**
> Executive Director of Lawyers' Committee on Nuclear Policy

QUESTIONS AND DEFINITIONS

1. What is the meaning of the statement "actions speak louder than words?" Is it true?

2. How often do you have great ideas but fail to act on them? What keeps you from taking action? What motivates you to act in spite of obstacles?

ACTIVITIES

 53.1 Use the quotes above as a foundation for a discussion for the role of an action in democracy and an action in your school and/or home community.

continued ▶

A C T I O N / ACTIVITIES, *continued*

 53.2 Study the life of Rosa Parks. Talk about the idea that one person's actions can make a difference.

 53.3 Journaling: Make a list of what you believe in; make a commitment to take action on one thing in which you believe. Make a list of the ways in which you can act on your belief and begin to make a difference.

 53.4 Use the Internet to learn about ending world hunger. Feed a hungry person in the world with the tap of a computer key by going to *www.thehungersite.com*.

 53.5 Draw a picture of an important event in your life in which what you did made a difference. Share your stories in class or on a visit to a children's center or convalescent home.

 53.6 What is the legacy that your class would like to leave to your school community? What action will you take to fulfill your legacy?

 53.7 What have people your own age done to make their community, or the world, a better place? How have they acted on behalf of human rights? How have they acted on behalf of the environment? *(For ideas, see Resources, pg. 167.)*

 53.8 Some people think that nonviolence means non-action. Write a short thought paper on how you would respond to that statement personally and strategically.
(See 198 nonviolent strategies for change at: www.aeinstein.org/ organizations103a.html)

 53.9 Select an example of organized nonviolent action such as the U.S. Sanctuary Movement, the Underground Railroad, Students Against Sweatshops, Justice for Janitors, or Amnesty International. What inspired these movements? What strategies were employed? How successful were they?

DAY 54

GIVING

Practice generosity by sharing time, energy and material resources with those in need. Clean out your closet, bureau drawers, or garage. Are there things you aren't using that might be of value to someone else? Today give away what you are no longer using.

QUOTE

Everything is given to me and I pass it on. You must give if you want to receive. Let the center of your being be one of giving, giving, giving. You can't give too much, and you will discover you cannot give without receiving. This kind of living is not reserved for the saints, but is available for the little people like you and me—if we reach out and give to everybody.

—Peace Pilgrim
Walked 25,000 miles for peace

We make a living by what we get. We make a life by what we give.
—Winston Churchill
British Prime Minister during World War II

The human contribution is the essential ingredient. It is only in the giving of oneself to others that we truly live.
—Ethel Percy Andrus
U.S. social activist (1884-1967)

QUESTIONS AND DEFINITIONS

1. What does it mean to "give of yourself?" What resources can you give that never run out?

2. What are you willing to give up in the name of peace?

3. What is the legacy that your class would like to give to your school community? What action will you take to fulfill your legacy?

GIVING / ACTIVITIES, *continued*

ACTIVITIES

 54.1 Imagine your life 50 years from now, and that you have been successful in all you have undertaken. Write an obituary highlighting your legacy—what you have given as your gift to others.

 54.2 As a class, give of your time and energy to promote active involvement in your school. Raise funds and donate a special bench, mural or other permanent structure on campus to remind others of your commitment to nonviolence.

 54.3 Make thank you cards and banners to honor those who helped promote the *64 Ways* campaign in your school. Invite them to a thank you ceremony and make presentations. Give back to others.

 54.4 Plan a presentation for your parents on what you have learned about nonviolence. Write a letter that will inspire them to visit the class. Present it to them at a parent-education evening.

 54.5 Plan a "give-away" ceremony to honor the giving of oral tradition. Participants all bring something that has held meaning for them that they are ready to pass on. Everything is placed anonymously in the center of the circle. Students walk around the circle silently and view the items. Everyone picks an item to which they are drawn. As students show what they have chosen around the circle, the giver reveals his or her identity and tells the story of his or her gift. (This is a wonderful exit activity for a group that has been working together for some time.)

 54.6 What can you give other than "things?" What else can you share? Make a class list.
1. Create coupons redeemable for one of these gifts.
2. Give at least one of these gifts each day for a week. Track your gift giving.
3. Journal about your experience—Tell about the effect your giving had on the receiver and the effect it had on the giver!

DAY 55

RESPONSIBILITY

The quality of your community starts with you. Take responsibility for the quality of your community wherever you are. Today, pick up trash that is not your own, whether at home, at the office, or on the street. Every little bit helps.

QUOTES

The salvation of this human world lies nowhere else than in the human heart, in the human power to reflect, in human meekness and in human responsibility.

—Vaclav Havel

Czech president

In our every deliberation, we must consider the impact of our decisions on the next seven generations.

—The Great Law of the Haudenosaunee

Six-Nation Iroquois Confederacy

In a world which presents such a dramatic struggle between life and death, the decisions we make about how to conduct our lives, about the kind of people we want to be have important consequences. In this context, one must stand on the side of life ... One works for justice not for the big victories, but simply because engaging in the struggle is itself worth doing.

—Oscar Arias Sanchez

Nobel Peace Laureate, Costa Rican president

QUESTIONS AND DEFINITIONS

1. Who is the most responsible person you know? How can you tell? What qualities do they have that you may want to embody?

2. How does taking responsibility differ from taking the blame?

3. Some people say that responsibility means, "the ability to respond rather than react." What does that mean? Do you agree?

4. In what areas of your life do you see yourself as responsible? In what areas do you feel you lack responsibility? Are there areas in which you feel you have too much responsibility for your age?

5. What makes people take on responsibility for community? What makes people hold back?

6. Talk about the eighth blunder of Gandhi's Eight Blunders: Rights without Responsibilities. What does that mean in a nation, for an individual, for you?

RESPONSIBILITY / ACTIVITIES, *continued*

ACTIVITIES

55.1 Share what kinds of responsibilities you have at home and how well you are at following through on them. Compare and contrast with the responsibilities you have at school. Why are these responsibilities important to the well-being of the household, school, you?

55.2 Read the Declaration of Independence. What are the responsibilities of the government to the people? What are the responsibilities of the people to the government? Write a thought paper. Create living sculptures to illustrate your findings.

55.3 We learn responsibility a little at a time. Starting at age three and continuing to the present, make an illustrated chart of the responsibilities you have assumed as you developed into the person you are now, from brushing your own teeth to watching younger siblings or driving a car. Construct a time-line of how your responsibilities have grown and changed as you have gotten older.

55.4 Draw a picture of the community in which you live. Include the people who take responsibility for the well being of the community in the picture. Who are they? What do they do? What are they like? Draw yourself into the picture. Where do you fit? What responsibilities do you take for the community? What responsibility could you take? What could you do today? Share pictures and post them around the room.

55.5 Research responsibilities of the people in a democracy. Evaluate how well we are fulfilling our responsibilities. Give examples. How can you and your peers begin to fulfill these responsibilities now? Do it.

55.6 Arun Gandhi added to his Grandfather's list of Blunders (on page A15), Rights without Responsibilities. Discuss the truth in this statement and how the two relate. Then write your own Bill of Rights and Responsibilities for your participation at home, at school, in your community or in your nation.

55.7 Choose and research an ecological issue being addressed in our culture today. Then write a script in which a character visits from the future with a message revealing the consequences of our actions seven generations down the line. You may have different groups of students address the same issue in different ways. What is our responsibility to the next seven generations? How well are we doing in fulfilling our responsibilities?

DAY 56

SELF-SUFFICIENCY

People need the dignity of work and the opportunity to provide for themselves and their families. Economic self-sufficiency is a requirement for a nonviolent world. Today, create a job for someone or help someone to find employment (Examples: Help them with a resume or application. Help them make phone calls, dress appropriately, practice interviewing).

QUOTES

Freedom is the greatest fruit of self-sufficiency.
—Aristotle
Greek physician and philosopher, student of Socrates (384-322 B.C.)

Happiness belongs to the self-sufficient.
—Epicurus
Greek philosopher, educator. (341-211 B.C.)

Interdependence is and ought to be as much the ideal of man as self-sufficiency.
—Gandhi
While leading Indian nonviolent resistance campaigns in South Africa

QUESTIONS AND DEFINITIONS

1. **What are the components of economic self-sufficiency?**

2. **How does it affect you when you are dependent rather than self-sufficient?**

3. **How does a person's economic self-sufficiency relate to their dignity and worth as a human being?**

4. **How does a community's or a nation's economic self-sufficiency relate to peace versus conflict? Share specific examples.**

5. **How can you be self-sufficient and still live at home? How does being self-sufficient relate to self-esteem?**

ACTIVITIES

56.1 What kinds of inner and outer "resources" are required for us to be successfully self-sufficient (e.g, education, community/friends, communication skills, professional and technical skills, self-mastery, income, etc.)? Can you be more self-sufficient in this resource? How?

continued ▶

SELF-SUFFICIENCY / ACTIVITIES, *continued*

 56.2 Could you be self-sufficient in the wild, without food or comforts? Investigate survival tactics for someone lost in the wilderness.

 56.3 Write a thought paper about personal self-sufficiency. What are the pros and cons of "standing on your own" as opposed to "being part of a group?" Which do you prefer? Must you be one or the other, or can you be both? What might that look like?

 56.4 What is required of a community of people in order to become economically self-sufficient? What must they do? What values are essential? What choices must they make? What skills must they develop?

 56.5 Boycotts have been a tool for nonviolent social change in many cultures. How did Indians in India, Africans in South Africa and African-Americans in the American South practice self-sufficiency during economic boycotts for equal rights? Explore a specific example of a country's efforts to be more self-sufficient (e.g., U.S. Boston Tea Party, a Third World country today).

DAY 57

SERVICE

Dr. Martin Luther King, Jr. said, "Everybody can be great, because anybody can serve. You only need a heart full of grace and a soul generated by love." Sign up to volunteer a minimum of two hours this month with an organization of your choice. Share your commitment with at least one person.

QUOTES

Service is the rent you pay for room on this Earth.
　　　　—**Congresswoman Shirley Chisholm**
　　　　　　First African-American woman elected to the U.S. Congress.

Never doubt that a small group of thoughtful committed citizens can change the world. Indeed it's the only thing that ever has.
　　　　—**Margaret Mead**
　　　　　　American anthropologist and writer (1901-1978)

We are questions for one another. And service is exploring and awakening through them.
　　　　—**Anonymous**

How wonderful it is that nobody need wait a single moment before starting to improve the world.
　　　　—**Anne Frank**
　　　　　　Her diary survived the Holocaust

The only politics I am willing to devote myself to is simply a matter of serving those around us: serving the community and serving those who will come after us. Its deepest roots are moral because it is a responsibility expressed through action, to and for the whole.
　　　　—**Vaclav Havel**
　　　　　　President of Czechoslovakia and the Czech Republic (b. 1936)

QUESTIONS AND DEFINITIONS

1. What is the definition of service?

2. How are you of service everyday to yourself, your family, your community?

3. In what community service activities have you participated? How does service affect the person giving the service?

4. Who stands out that has been of service to you? What did they do? What qualities did they express? What made their service stand out in your mind?

5. Why is service an important principle of nonviolence? What role does attitude play in service?

continued ▶

SERVICE / QUESTIONS

ACTIVITIES

 57.1 Being of service is said to be a gift for the giver as well as the receiver. Where can you be of service today? Choose one thing you will accomplish at home, at school, or in the community. Write about how it felt to surprise someone with the gift of your service.

 57.2 Choose tasks around the classroom that you can do to serve the whole class. Make a sign up sheet and continue to carry out these tasks for the rest of the year.

 57.3 Provide service for another classroom by offering to tutor or read to younger students, or to help correct papers. Service assists us in appreciating another's work. How does the person giving service benefit? Have participants journal about their experience and highlights.

 57.4 Adopt a community service project for your class to work on together for the rest of the semester. Debrief at the end of the project. Has the class benefited from this experience? Hold a class council to reflect on memories and stories. What was the most important aspect of your experience?

 57.5 Research the work of a Nobel Peace Laureate, Doctors without Borders, the work of Mother Teresa, Dorothy Day, Princess Diana, Ari Ariyaratne, or the Columbian Children's Peace Movement. What part did service play in their lives? Write a monologue to praise the work of the individual you select.

DAY 58

CITIZENSHIP

Robert Muller, former assistant secretary general to the UN, urges, "Use every letter you write, every conversation you have, every meeting you attend, to express your fundamental beliefs and dreams." Today call or write one of your legislators and register your views.

QUOTES

To be a citizen is to transform society.
—Augusto Boal
Brazilian educator, dramatist

Without free, self-respecting, and autonomous citizens there can be no free and independent nations. Without internal peace, that is, peace among citizens and between the citizens and the state, there can be no guarantee of external peace.
—Vaclav Havel
Leader of the democratic Civic Forum,
key figure in the Velvet Revolution

Do we mock democracy each time we back away, each time we fail to participate actively in the struggles for transformation of our institutions and of this nation, in the defense of the poor, in the protection of the environment, in the question of our political leaders, in the teaching of ourselves and our children … ?
—Vincent Harding
Author, associate of Dr. Martin Luther King, Jr.

I have said that the Declaration of Independence is the ringbolt to the chain of your nation's destiny; so, indeed, I regard it. The principles contained in that instrument are saving principles. Stand by those principles, be true to them on all occasions, in all places, against all foes, and at whatever cost.
—Frederick Douglass
A Leader of the U.S. Abolitionist movement (1818-1895)

QUESTIONS AND DEFINITIONS

1. What does citizenship mean?

2. What do you think the rights and responsibilities of citizenship are?

3. What kind of citizen do you think you are in this country? What kind of citizen are you in your school? In your community? Why are you that kind of citizen?

4. Is citizenship important? If there are students in class who are not citizens, invite them to express their views.

5. What does Muller's quote, in the box above, mean to you?

CITIZENSHIP / ACTIVITIES, *continued*

ACTIVITIES

 58.1 Express your citizenship today by writing letters to a member of the Congress, or a member of the State Assembly on a current topic of interest to your community. Each student's letter may express his or her personal view on the topic. Notice how we do not all have to agree to be active citizens.

 58.2 Invite a newly naturalized American citizen to speak with your class. Invite them to share what made them become a citizen.

 58.3 Learn about the children of Columbia who changed the course of their country's future with their intense commitment to citizenship. See the video *Soldiers of Peace* (See *Nonviolence Videos*, pg. 181).

 58.4 Good citizenship requires that you be informed. Have the group identify an issue they care about and invite speakers to address the class. Prepare questions. Dialogue about what you learned and what action you will take. Take the action and write about the result.

 58.5 Select a community or national issue that is currently being considered for a vote. Create a mock election for candidates or a ballot initiative. Plan a debate by the candidates or a panel discussion on the issue and then take the vote. Discuss what points brought you to your decision? Debrief this activity by brainstorming the ways, both pro and con, in which citizens are swayed and influenced in the voting process.

DAY 59

INTERVENTION

The use of alcohol, tobacco and drugs all have consequences and cause personal and public violence. Today, have the courage to intervene in a caring way with someone whose behavior is destructive. Through your honest, direct, and loving communication, encourage them to get help, get educated, get sober, and get free.

QUESTIONS AND DEFINITIONS

1. **What is an intervention? How does it work?**

2. **When has someone intervened in your life to help you get back on track? Was the intervention successful?**

3. **Have you ever intervened on someone else's behalf? Were you successful? How did you feel?**

4. **When is it important to speak up on another's behalf?**

ACTIVITIES

 59.1 The most common interventions we first experience come about when our parents or guardians set standards and house rules. Write a paper on some of your house rules and how your parents have intervened in some cases to keep you out of harm's way. What did they do? How did you respond? What was the outcome?

 59.2 One of the most common organizational interventions takes place in 12-step programs for people experiencing drug or alcohol abuse. Have a speaker from your local AA or NA come to talk to your class about intervention. Review how drug and alcohol abuse relate to violence against one's self and others. Consider how recovery can promote nonviolence.

 59.3 Have students write a confidential thought paper in which they answer the following questions: Do you know someone who needs help? Are you willing to talk to them today and tell them the truth as you see it? Are you willing to talk about the situation with an adult you trust? What does it mean to care enough to tell the truth? What stops people from intervening? Who is responsible for what?

 59.4 Create a comic strip of an intervention that prevented a disastrous outcome.

59.5 Brainstorm the ways in which nonviolent action serves as community intervention. Are there examples in your own community in which citizens who took a stand prevented a detrimental outcome? What nonviolent strategies did they employ?

(Refer to The Politics of Nonviolent Action by Gene Sharp. See Adult Bibliography, pg. 172)

DAY 60

WITNESSING

"We are each other's bond," writes poet Gwendolyn Brooks. Those who practice nonviolence cannot close their eyes to injustice or cruelty. We are here to be a witness for justice and compassion. Today be willing to stand up for truth by your presence, your words and actions.

QUOTE

Interviewer: "How can we bear witness to the lacerating effects of treachery, betrayal, abandonment, so much a part of our ordinary world?"
Joan Halifax: "How can we not?"
—*Peacemaker* Magazine (February 2000)

QUESTIONS AND DEFINITIONS

1. When someone "bears witness" in a culture of nonviolence, they are present to observe and document an event or an experience so that what happens is not forgotten. There is personal testimony, video, radio, etc. that documents what has taken place. Sometimes people serve as witnesses to an election to say whether or not the election is honest and fair, to discourage the intimidation or influencing of a citizen's vote. Sometimes a witness escorts people in danger, with the belief that a witness discourages violence and illegal or immoral action. Sometimes a witness listens and records the experiences of others, so that the experience of another human being is honored and the importance of an event is acknowledged. Sometimes the mere presence of a witness can influence and prevent violence.

2. Have you ever acted as a witness for a ceremony or court proceeding? What was your responsibility?

3. What would you do if you witnessed, in person, a violent act at school, or if you witnessed someone talking about a violent action that was being planned?

4. How does it feel to witness an act of fairness? How does it feel to witness an act of injustice?

ACTIVITIES

60.1 Usually we connect the idea of a witness to a crime. However, we can be witness to wonderful events as well. Think of a time when you witnessed an unexpected, wonderful event. Report what you saw with all of the details as though you are a journalist.

60.2 Interview an older person about an important event in their lives (e.g. ask them questions like: "What is an event that has greatly influenced the person you are today?", or "What is an important event in history that greatly affected you?"). Be a witness for their unique human experience. Use the skills you have been learning as a practitioner of nonviolence to be a deep listener and an excellent witness for their experience. Share their story. Share your experience.

continued ▶

WITNESSING / ACTIVITIES, *continued*

 60.3 In groups, identify an event that has happened in your community that had a great impact. Have each member of the group gather testimony (either in written, audio, video or photographic format) from at least one person who "witnessed" the event. Create a journal, web page, newspaper article, or radio show using the gathered testimony from the witness.

 60.4 Witnessing can take many forms. Learn about diverse expressions of witnessing by reading and studying the following:
    a. Witness for Peace, Witness.org, Global Witness, International Peace Brigades
    b. *Twilight*, Anna Devere Smith (One woman show about the Los Angeles 1991 uprising)
    c. The Listening Project (Middle East)
    d. The AIDS Quilt
    e. Truth and Reconciliation Commission in South Africa
    f. Peace Pilgrim
    g. Million Man March
    h. Mothers of Plaza de Mayo
Write a paper on one of the above listings, and present the paper to the class.

 60.5 For Mature Students Only in groups, research on the Web organizations that bear witness for peace (i.e. Witness for Peace, International Peace Brigades, United Nations and Carter Center election monitors). How have their efforts made a contribution to peace? Invite a representative of your group to share their experiences.

DAY 61

PEACE

An 11 year old wrote, "Peace is a special thought or a special love or light or spark that we all share within ourselves." Thich Nhat Hanh wrote, "Practice watering seeds of joy and peace and not just seeds of anger and violence, and the elements of war in all of us will be transformed." Today, make a choice to meet each experience with an intention for peace.

QUOTES

Once peace is made within, one will have gained sufficient strength and power to use in the struggle of life, both within and without.

—Hazrat Inayat Khan
Indian teacher who brought Sufism to the West (1882-1927)

Peace is not the product of terror or fear. Peace is not the silence of cemeteries. Peace is not the silent result of violent repression. Peace is the generous, tranquil contribution of all to the good of all. Peace is dynamism. Peace is generosity. It is right and it is duty.

—Archbishop Oscar Romero
El Savadorean Catholic educator, human rights activist,
champion of the poor, assassinated in 1980

QUESTIONS AND DEFINITIONS

1. Describe the most peaceful memory you have. How old were you? Where were you and what were you doing?

2. What is peace: the absence of something or the presence of something?

3. What would it mean to find "real peace?" What is necessary for peace?

4. Is peace possible?

5. What is the role of the individual in creating peace in the world?

6. Is there peace that no one can take away from you? Learn about people who have found peace in jail, in war and in suffering. Where did they find that peace? How did they find it?

ACTIVITIES

 61.1 Plan a period of peace for your class. Choose an outdoor location if possible or an indoor space with comfortable seating. Play some soothing music, do a guided imagery meditation and travel (in your mind's eye) to an environment that is peaceful for you. Describe the peaceful place to which you have traveled. What does it look like, feel like, taste like? What kinds of things are in the environment? What and who is there with you? What are you doing? Let yourself be surprised by the images that are revealed.

continued ▶

P E A C E / ACTIVITIES, *continued*

 61.2 Plant a peace garden and watch it grow. What makes it a peace garden? How does tending a peace garden compare to tending peace in your own life in the world?

 61.3 Make a peace quilt. Have each student design their own square.

 61.4 Divide the class into groups of four and five students and have each group of students create their own Peace Expression Project. Let students use writing, music, performance, poetry, art and any other means that they choose.

 61.5 Have the class write "peace news" headlines for the school paper, a community paper, or the television news (e.g. Peace Broke Out or Countries Unite). What would they like to announce to the world? Have each student write what they saw, heard, smelled, etc.

 61.6 What is the Nobel Peace Prize? How was the award established? Have each member of the class select a Nobel Peace Prize recipient to research and then write a three-page report about his or her life. Include information on accomplishments, personal qualities and what inspired them to do what they did to become an honoree. After each student has presented his or her report to the class, debrief this activity by reflecting on the qualities and commonalities of these individuals.

 61.7 Find an inspirational quote about peace that speaks to you. Allow the quote to inspire you, and create an artistic (visual presentation) that includes the quote. As the work is presented to the class, discuss any feelings you may have discovered while completing this project.

 61.8 Write a story in the third person about someone your age who is involved in peacemaking. What did they do? How did they do it? Were they effective in their peacemaking efforts? If so, why? If not, how could they have been more effective?

61.9.1 Write seven things you have learned about yourself during this study of nonviolence. Write seven things you learned about peacemaking.

61.9.2 Make a poster that represents peacemaking or the practice of nonviolence, and incorporate your list of seven things above into the poster.

61.9.3 Write a journal entry about what Peace has come to mean to you in your own life, in your community, your country, and in the world.

DAY 62

COMMITMENT

Spend five minutes reflecting on your commitment to nonviolence. Write down what it means to you to be committed to nonviolence, and what you are willing to do as a demonstration of your commitment.

QUOTES

Until one is committed there is hesitancy, the chance to draw back, always ineffectiveness. Concerning all acts of initiative (and creation) there is one elementary truth, the ignorance of which kills countless ideas and splendid plans; the moment one definitely commits oneself, then Providence moves too. All sorts of things occur to help one that would otherwise never have occurred. A whole stream of events issues from the decision, raising in one's favor all manner of unforeseen incidents and meetings and material assistance, which no man could have dreamed would have come his way.

—W.N. Murray
Of the Scottish Himalayan Expedition

We mutually pledge to each other our lives, our fortunes, and our sacred honour.
—Thomas Jefferson
Author of the Declaration of Independence

QUESTIONS AND DEFINITIONS

1. What is a commitment and how do you honor your commitments? How can you tell when someone is committed? How would you evaluate your follow through in regard to your commitment?

2. What commitments have you made to yourself and others?

3. What values are you truly committed to in your life that can be witnessed through your actions?

4. What is your commitment to nonviolence?

5. Has your commitment to nonviolence as a way of life changed or grown over the past few weeks? If it has grown, reflect on how it has grown, and share your findings with the class.

COMMITMENT / ACTIVITIES

ACTIVITIES

 62.1 Divide the class into triads. Tell each other what you believe about nonviolence and what your commitment is. How will you practice it? Witness for each other.

 62.2 Interview one of your personal heroes of nonviolence and find out how commitment has played a role in his or her life.

 62.3 Write a poem or piece of prose that begins with the line, "When there is commitment ..." Explore such things as how it might change one's actions, how it makes one feel, what it looks like and how the world responds to it. Use metaphor, alliteration and descriptive language.

 62.4 Have the class create a contract for peace and circulate it on campus so others may sign it. Make copies to distribute and display.

 62.5 Research and write about the role that commitment has played in the lives of a hero for human rights and dignity (e.g. Sadako Sasaki, Chiune Sugihara, Anne Frank, suffragettes like Susan B. Anthony and Jane Addams, the Chipko Tree Huggers of India, Ruby Bridges or Fannie Lou Hamer, Julia Butterfly Hill or Albert Bigelow).

 62.6 A myth is a supernatural, magical or religious legend or story that is based on a particular culture and that seeks to explain something about the way the world or the society works, "why things are the way they are." Research the tradition of myths. Invite teams of students to create myths about peace/ nonviolence and commitment. Write, act, create music and poetry in order to share your myth.

DAY 63

RELEASE

A Sufi proverb says, "When the heart weeps for what it has lost, the spirit laughs for what it has found." Today look back on how far you have come during this 64 day journey. Release the weight of your past judgments of yourself and others, and release the idea that world peace is not possible. Acknowledge that you do make a difference!

QUOTES

Am I willing to give up what I have in order to be what I am not yet? Am I willing to let my ideas of myself, of humanity, be changed? Am I able to follow the spirit of love into the desert, to empty myself even of my concept of emptiness?

—M. C. Richards
Poet (1916-1999)

QUESTIONS AND DEFINITIONS

1. What does it mean to release an old way of thinking?

2. How does holding on to the past limit us (i.e., excessively weeping for what we have lost)?

3. How can you release the past with regard to nonviolence?

4. What do you need to release in order to be the person you want to be.

ACTIVITIES

63.1 Identify something that you are holding on to from your past. Write down on a small piece of paper what you have identified. Clench the paper tightly in your fist.

Sentence completion exercise: "Write down at least five different endings to the following phrase: "I'm holding on so tight that . . ." Choose a partner and tell him or her some of the qualities you would like to experience once you let go of the past. Your partner will write down those qualities for you on small pieces of paper.

Clinch your fist. Let your partner offer you the qualities on the pieces of paper, one by one, and each time they offer, relax, and when you are ready, release and let go, unclenching your fist and opening your hand to receive what they offer. Become aware that as you hold on to the past tightly, you cannot accept the good that is here now.

Be mindful of how much energy it takes to keep your fist tightly clenched. Think of all the things you can't do because you only have one hand free.

Complete the sentence: "As I release, I am free to . . ." Write down at least five different endings to this sentence. Share your experience.

continued ▶

RELEASE / ACTIVITIES, *continued*

 63.2 Release an old grudge. Write a short paper about something that has happened and about which you are holding a grudge. Forgive yourself and those involved. Read your paper to the class. Then tear the paper into pieces to symbolize your intention to move on.

 63.3 Do a drawing that includes words and phrases of old judgments and ideas that you are ready to release. What are you ready to embrace in their place? Shout it out!

63.4 Make flash cards of the principles of nonviolence discussed in the *64 Ways*, and play charades using the cards. Have the students guess which "way"—which principle—is being acted out. Recognize how the principles overlap.

DAY 64

CELEBRATION

Rejoice in the work that you have done. Celebrate the journey that you have made with countless others who believe that every individual can move the world in the direction of peace with their nonviolent choice and action. Margaret Mead said, "Never doubt that a small group of thoughtful committed citizens can change the world; indeed, it is the only thing that ever has."

QUOTES

When you look back on your life, you should have changed the world somehow.

—Senal Sarihan
Turkish attorney and human rights advocate

The time of the lone wolf is over. Gather yourselves; banish the word "struggle" from your attitude and vocabulary. All that we do now must be done in a sacred way and in celebration. We are the ones we've been waiting for.

—Hopi Elder
Oraibi, Arizona

It is good to have an end to journey towards; but it is the journey that matters, in the end.

—Ursula K. LeGuin
Science fiction and fantasy author

QUESTIONS AND DEFINITIONS

1. What kinds of celebrations do we participate in all the time? What is your favorite way to celebrate?

2. What does celebration have to do with "rites of passage?" Why are both important in our lives?

3. Which cultural celebrations are you familiar with? Have you participated in a celebration of a culture different than your own? What did you observe? What was your experience?

ACTIVITIES

 64.1 Bring in magazines and mementos to create a huge collage or an art installation to celebrate all the elements of nonviolence that you have recognized, discovered and learned during the last 64 days.

continued ▶

CELEBRATION / ACTIVITIES, *continued*

 64.2 Create a class ritual to celebrate your accomplishments and commitment to nonviolence.

 64.3 Have students create a scrapbook or make a video including class writings, art, photographs and other documentation of the collective experience over the *64 Ways* campaign.

 64.4 Put together an assembly for the whole school, having each class participate in a way that represents their experience, unique style and future commitment to nonviolence. Encourage students to include elements of the different cultures and ethnic backgrounds represented in the class.

64.5 Share about and enjoy how far you have come in studying the *64 Ways to Practice Nonviolence*. Give each student an opportunity to reflect and assess how they have been affected/changed by participating in the nonviolence campaign. How has the class been affected/changed? How has the school been affected/changed? Celebrate the growth and change!

NONVIOLENCE RESOURCES

PROGRAMS AND MATERIALS

American Friends Service Committee

www.afsc.org
AFSC National Office
1501 Cherry Street
Philadelphia, PA 19102
Phone: (215) 241-7000
Fax: (215) 241-7275
Email: afscinfo@afsc.org

Anti-Defamation League

www.adl.org
L.A. Regional Office Contact Info
(address not given)
Email: los-angeles@adl.org@adl.org
Phone: (310) 446-8000
Fax: (310) 470-8712
For Regional Offices
http://www.adl.org/main_regional.asp

Center for Council Training

www.centerforcounciltraining.org
c/o The Ojai Foundation
9739 Ojai-Santa Paula Road
Ojai, CA 93023
Phone: (805) 646-8343
E-Mail: program@ojaifoundation.org.

Children's Defense Fund

Marion Wright Edelman, Director
www.children'sdefensefund.org
25 E. Street, N.W.
NW Washington, DC 20001

Common Peace, Center for the Advancement of Nonviolence

www.nonviolenceworks.com
Candace Carnicelli, Director
1223 Wilshire Blvd., #472
Santa Monica, CA 90403
Phone: (323) 931-9125
Fax: (818) 936-0573

Days of Respect Program

Ralph J. Cantor
Innovations in Learning
2808 Hillegass Avenue
Berkeley, CA 94705
(501) 845-9494

Educating for Diversity

Office of Intergroup Relations
L.A. Unified School District
450 N. Grand Ave., Room P-318
Los Angeles, CA 90012
(213) 625-6579

Facing History and Ourselves

www.facinghistory.org
16 Hurd Road
Brookline, MA 02146
(617) 232-1595
(617) 232-0281
L.A. Regional Office
1276 E. Colorado Blvd. Suite 207
Pasadena, CA 91106
(626) 744-1177

NONVIOLENCE RESOURCES

PROGRAMS AND MATERIALS

Families Against Violence Advocacy Network

> www.membersaol.com/ppjn
> c/o Institute for Peace and Justice
> 4144 Lindell Blvd. #408
> St. Louis, MO 63108
> (314) 533-4445
> E-mail: ppjn@aol.com
> Parenting for Peace and Justice
>   Newsletter available

Fellowship of Reconciliation

> www.forusa.org
> National Headquarters
> 521 N. Broadway
> Nyack, New York 10960
> 845-358-4601

The Free Child Project

> www.freechild.org
> 407 Adams Street
> Suite 215
> Olympia, Washington, USA 98501
> Phone: (360) 753-2686

International Youth Parliament

> www.youthparliament.org
> Oxfam Community Aid Abroad
> International Coordinator, Brett Solomon
> Program Coordinator, Sofiah Mackay
> GPO Box 1000
> Sydney NSW 1043
> Australia
> Phone: 61-2-8204-3900
> Fax: 61-2-9280-3426
> Email: info@iyp.oxfam.org

Jampolsky Outreach Foundation

> www.wethepeople.org
> P.O. Box 1057
> Larkspur, CA 94977
> Phone: (415) 461-0500
> Fax (415) 925-0330
> E-Mail: pathways@peacenet.org.

M.K. Gandhi Institute

> www.gandhiinstitute.org
> Arun Gandhi, Founder & Director
> 650 East Parkway South
> Memphis, TN 38104

National Conference for Community and Justice

> www.nccj.org/national
> 475 Park Avenue South, 19th Floor
> New York, NY 10016
> Phone: (212) 545-1300
> Fax: (212) 545-8053
> Email: nationaloffice@nccj.org
> L.A. Regional Office
> Fran Spears, Executive Director
> 3000 Olympic Blvd.
> Santa Monica, CA 90404
> Phone: (310) 315-4801
> Fax: (310) 315-4807

Nonviolence.Org.

> www.nonviolence.org
> What one man, Marin Kelley Ranter, has done with his entirely virtual new media organization

NONVIOLENCE RESOURCES

PROGRAMS AND MATERIALS

Nuclear Age Peace Foundation

www.wagingpeace.org.
PMB121, 1187 Coast Village Road Suite 1
Santa Barbara, CA 93108-2794
Phone: (805) 965-3443
Fax: (805) 568-0466

Pace E Bene Franciscan Center

2901 Channing Way
Berkeley, CA 94704-2506
Attention: Ken Butigan
(410) 549-0130
E-mail: beatitude@compuserve.com

Paul Kivel

Violence Prevention Educator
658 Vernon Street
Oakland, CA. 94610
pkivel@mindspring.com
www.paulkivel.com
Phone: (510) 654-3015

Pax Christi

www.paxchristi.com
12100 Pioneer Trail
Eden Praire, MN 55347-4208
Phone: (952) 941-3150
Fax: (952) 941-7942

Peace and Justice Resource Center

E-mail: LPF@ecunet.org
Contact: Glen Gersmehl
1710 – 11th Ave.
Seattle, Washington 98122
Phone: (206) 720-0313

A Season for Nonviolence

Barbara Bernstein, Executive Director
www.seasonfornonviolence-cs.org
www.agnt.org
Association for Global New Thought
220 Santa Anita Road
Santa Barbara, CA 93105
Phone: (805) 563-7343
Fax (805) 563-7344
Email: Barbara@agnt.org

Teaching Tolerance

www.tolerance.org
A Project of Southern Poverty Law Center
www.splc.com
400 Washington Ave.
Montgomery, AL 36104
Phone: (334) 264-3121
Fax: (334) 264-7310
Teaching Tolerance Magazine available

Touch The Earth Foundation

E-mail: Kcb4behopi@aol.com
P.O. Box 257
Solano Beach, CA 92075
Phone: (619) 481-9824

Youth Activism Project

www.youthactivism.com
P.O. Box E
Kensington, MD, 20895
Phone: 1-800-KID-POWER
E-mail: info@youthactivism.com

NONVIOLENCE RESOURCES

ADULT BIBLIOGRAPHY

Anti-Defamation League
Close The Book On Hate: 101 Ways to Combat Prejudice
> There is the opportunity to make "A World of Difference" in this thin pamphlet. Definitions, response strategies to bigotry and intolerance, ways to plan for hate crimes as a school or community as well as the 101 ways to combat prejudice are provided here in an accessible format.
> New York: Anti-Defamation League, 1998

Carnes, Jim, editor
Teaching Tolerance Magazine
> This magazine provides a wealth of information, and inspiration in the struggle for peace through justice and equality for all.
> Southern Poverty Law Center, 2001

Chapple, Christopher Key
Nonviolence to Animals, Earth, and Self in Asian Traditions
> This book probes the origins of the practice of nonviolence in early India and traces its path within the Jaina, Hindu, and Buddhist traditions, including its impact on East Asia. It then turns to a variety of contemporary issues relating to nonviolence, such as vegetarianism, animal and environmental protection, and the cultivation of religious tolerance.
> Albany: State University of New York Press., 1993

Coles, Robert
The Moral Intelligence of Children: How To Raise A Moral Child
> The author, a Harvard Medical School professor of psychiatry and medical humanities, writes a powerful book, exploring ways parents and teachers can foster generosity of spirit and empathy in children.
> New York: Random House, Inc., 1997

Corkille Briggs, Dorothy
Your Child's Self-Esteem
> In this timeless classic, a most important characteristic in the developing child, the feeling of self-worth, is explained, nurtured and illuminated. The reader learns ways to facilitate positive self-esteem, creating an environment of tolerance for all.
> New York: Doubleday, 1970

Creighton, Allan, Battered Women's Alternatives, with Paul Kivel, Oakland Men's Project
Helping Teens Stop Violence
> This workbook will assist teachers in facilitating high school youth in understanding and addressing violence that affects teens directly; includes strategies, curriculum plans, guidelines for effective adult support
> Alameda: Hunter House, 1990

NONVIOLENCE RESOURCES

ADULT BIBLIOGRAPHY

Cummins, Paul F.
Two Americas, Two Educations

> This book grapples with the long unanswered question of what is in the way of America providing quality education to our children. It reveals the injustices that are suffered by our children, our families and our Nation as a result of inadequate finance and funding in our educational systems. It tells America what it needs to do in order to successfully move from offering "adequate" to "superior" education.
> Los Angeles: Red Hen Press, 2006

Dear, John, editor
Mohandas Gandhi, Essential Writings

> John Dear, a Jesuit priest and veteran of many nonviolent campaigns, collected these particular works by Gandhi. They shed light on the essential principles and spiritual foundation upon which Gandhi built his life and work.
> New York: Orbis Books, 2002

Gandhi, Mohanndas K.
An Autobiography: The Story of Experiments with Truth

> Gandhi recounts the story of his life and shares with the reader how he developed the concept of Satyagraha—active, nonviolent resistance. His life and writings are a testament to the strength of spirit.
> Boston: Beacon Press, 1993

Gandhi, Mohanndas K.
Non-Violent Resistance (Satyagraha)

> Nonviolent resistance (satyagraha) is defined in Gandhi's own words, in terms of the personal discipline and code of conduct, nonviolent strategy of resistance, specific campaigns in the Indian struggle and as a basis for social reform. This is a "textbook" that codifies the practice of satyagraha—"clinging to Truth."
> New York: Schocken Books, 1961

Gandhi, Arun
Legacy of Love: My Education in the Path of Nonviolence

> Arun Gandhi's memoirs of lessons that he learned from his grandfather, Mohandas Gandhi, and his parents about the power and workings of nonviolence.
> El Sobrante, California: North Bay Books, 2003

Halberstrom, David
The Children

> Martin Luther King, Jr. recruits Rev. James L. Lawson to come to Nashville and train students in Gandhian techniques of nonviolence. They become leaders in the Nashville sit-ins, the Freedom Rides, SCLC and SNCC; they go on to become leaders in our country.
> London: Random House, 1998

NONVIOLENCE RESOURCES

ADULT BIBLIOGRAPHY

Helder, John
The Tao of Leadership: Leadership Strategies for a New Age
> A discourse on leadership strategies based on the principles of the Tao Te Ching by Lao Tsu.
> Humanics Limited, Atlanta, GA: Bantam Press, 1985

Males, Mike
The Scapegoat Generation: America's War on Adolescents
> Males advocates for today's youth generation with regard to violence, drug addiction, and the 'bad rap' he
> determines they are receiving from baby boomers.
> Monroe, ME: Common Cause Press, 1996

Rosenberg, Marshall B
Nonviolent Communication: A Language of Compassion,
> Teachers, counselors and students can learn verbal skills that promote empathy and help prevent misunder
> standing and violence, in the easy-to-follow format of this book.
> Del Mar, CA: Puddle Dancer Press, 1999

Sauerwein, Leigh
The Way Home
> These ethnically diverse short stories revolve around the theme of freedoms lost and found. Included are
> issues related to slavery, family and self-discovery and disability.
> New York: Farrar, Strauss & Giroux, 1994.

Sharp, Gene
The Politics of Nonviolent Action
> The definitive history and analysis of nonviolence as a strategy for change, including 198 strategies
> Boston: Porter Sargent Publisher, 1973

Singer, Bennett L., editor
Growing Up Gay/Growing Up Lesbian
> Themes, including friendship, self-discovery, family and interacting with the world, are explored in this book.
> Excerpts from noted gay and lesbian authors, journal entries and essays from teens round out this anthology.
> New York: New Press, 1994

Waller, James
Prejudice Across America
> Highly acclaimed, this book tells the true story of a professor and his students' nationwide trek toward
> racial understanding.
> Jackson: University Press of Mississippi, 2000

NONVIOLENCE RESOURCES

ADULT BIBLIOGRAPHY

Zimmerman, Jack and Virginia Coyle
The Way of Council
> This book offers insightful reflections from teachers, students and council facilitators on the use of council circles, to develop communication skills and build community.
> Las Vegas, NV: Bramble Press, 1996

Zinn, Howard
A People's History of the United States
> A chronicle of American history that tells the American story from the point of view of—and in the words of—America's women, factory workers, African American, Native Americans, the working poor, and immigrant laborers. Many of the country's greatest battles—the fights for a fair wage, an eight-hour workday, child-labor laws, health and safety standards, universal suffrage, women's rights, racial equality—were carried out at a grassroots level.
> New York: HarperCollins, 1999

NONVIOLENCE RESOURCES

STUDENT BIBLIOGRAPHY

HIGH SCHOOL

Conly, Jane Leslie
Crazy Lady
> When Vernon gets a new tutor, he learns much about tolerance from the alcoholic woman and her mentally impaired son that he and his friends have been teasing.
> New York: HarperCollins, 1993

Richard J. Jensen, John C. Hammerback
The Words of Cesar Chavez
> A collection of writings by Caesar Chavez.
> Texas A&M University Press, 2002

Martin Luther King, Jr., edited by Clayborne Carson
Autobiography of Martin Luther King, Jr.
> Clayborne Carson, the director the Martin Luther King papers Project, weaves together the writings, speeches letters, etc. of Martin Luther King, Jr. to create an intimate and moving autobiography of the Nobel Peace Laureate.
> New York: Warner Books, 2001

Easwaran, Eknath
Gandhi the Man
> A highly readable biography of Gandhi with many photographs and quotes.
> Tomales: Nilgiri Press, 1972

Easwaran, Eknath
Nonviolent Soldier of Islam: Badshah Khan, A Man to Match His Mountains
> Abdul Ghaffar Khan was Muslim leader of Pathan people on India's northwest frontier and ally of Mohanndas K. Gandhi in the nonviolent struggle for Indian Independence. From the most fierce Pathan warriors, he raised history's first nonviolent army of 100,000 men.
> Tomales: Nilgiri Press, 1984

Gold, Alison Leslie Gold
A Special Fate: Chiune Sugihara, Hero of the Holocaust
> Japanese diplomat, Chiune Sugihara, disobeyed orders and saved the lives of thousands of Jews during World War II.
> Lindfield: Scholastic Press, 2000

Houston, Jeanne Wakatsuki and James D.
Farewell to Manzanar
> In 1942, Jeanne Wakatsuki was seven years old. It was during this time that she and her family, along with 10,000 other Japanese Americans, were uprooted from their homes and sent to live at Manzanar internment camp. This book is the true story of Jeanne's family life. It is a classic, which captures the indignities suffered by people, who were forced to leave behind property, businesses, friends and perhaps the trust of other Americans purely because of race. The story also illuminates the resilience of the human spirit when true identity is known, despite treatment received.
> New York: Bantam Books, 1973

NONVIOLENCE RESOURCES

STUDENT BIBLIOGRAPHY

Ingraham, Catherine
In the Footsteps of Gandhi: Conversations with Spiritual Social Activists
> Interviews with 12 leaders of nonviolence including the Dalai Lama, Desmond Tutu, Murabek Awad, Joan Baez, Joanna Macy and more …
> Berkeley: Parallax Press, 1990

Katz, William Loren and Franklin, Paul A.
Proudly Red and Black: Stories of African and Native Americans
> In these six lively biographies, readers see how unique heritage serves as a source of pride and empowerment when discrimination and oppression are confronted.
> New York: Atheneum, 1993

Khamisa, Azim with Goldman, Carl
Azim's Bardo: A Father's Journey From Murder to Forgiveness
> In this moving story, we learn about the depth of forgiveness. It is with an immense commitment to the concept of restorative justice (seeking to restore wholeness to victims and communities when crimes are committed, including the opportunity for perpetrators to redeem themselves, in part, by becoming contributing, responsible members of society) that Azim Khamisa and Ples Felix embark on their heartfelt journey of healing.
> Los Altos: Rising Star Press, 1998

Khong, Sister Chan
Learning True Love: How I Learned to Practice Social Change in Vietnam
> Autobiography of a woman of inspirational courage—an intimate perspective on the suffering of the Vietnamese people, her experiences during the Vietnam war, her personal journey of peace-making and helping humanity; insights into the life and teachings of Thich Nhat Hanh, Nobel peace nominee.
> Berkeley, Parallax Press, 1993

King Jr., Martin Luther
Where Do We Go From Here: Chaos or Community?
> A book of Martin Luther King, Jr. essays that eloquently articulate his vision for America, the practice of nonviolence and the challenges before us.
> New York: Harper & Row, Publishers, 1967

James Melvin Washington (Editor), Martin Luther King, Jr.
A Testament of Hope
> The Essential Writings and Speeches of Martin Luther King, Jr.
> Harper: San Francisco, 1991

NONVIOLENCE RESOURCES

STUDENT BIBLIOGRAPHY

Lee, Harper
To Kill A Mockingbird

> The story of racial bigotry and salvation unfolds as innocently as children playing on a warm summer day. Family relationships, loss and a child's attempt to explore and expand her world alongside others are juxtaposed with a moving case of injustice, which results in lessons for all.
> New York: Warner Books, Inc., 1960

Lowry, Lois
The Giver

> No music, no color, no differences. These are some of the characteristics of one boy's world. In this touching story, the boy tries to solve the problems of his world one step at a time.
> New York: Bantam Doubleday Dell, 1993

Menchu Tum, Rigoberta
I, Rigoberta Menchu: An Indian Woman In Guatamala

> From peasant to Nobel Peace Laureate, this is the autobiography of an heroic woman and the struggle of the indigenous people of Guatemala for human rights, freedom and dignity.
> London: Verso, 1984

Milkman, Ruth and Kent Wong
Voices from the Front Lines: Organizing Immigrant Workers in Los Angeles

> Autobiographical sketches of five immigrant workers who found their voices as organizers and leaders in the labor movement in Los Angeles; in English and Spanish.
> Los Angeles: UCLA Center for Labor Research and Education, 2000

Myers, Walter Dean
Monster

> The compelling account of a 16 year old male, accused of being an accomplice to a murder, who records his experiences in court and in prison in the form of a film script, giving the reader a unique and intimate view of this time in the life of a teen.
> Harper Collins Publishers, Inc., 1999

Opdyke, Irene Gut with Armstrong, Jennifer
In My Hands: Memories of a Holocaust Rescuer

> Irene Opdyke was a sixteen year old Catholic teen in Poland in 1939, when she was beaten and left for dead by soldiers. This memoir is her story; the story of a non-Jew, one of many, who risked her life day after day to save the lives of those Hitler was determined to exterminate. Her devotion to resistance of what was wrong was also a testament to her belief in humanity.
> New York: Anchor Books, 1999

Stern-LaRosa, Caryl and Bettmann, Ellen Hofheimer
The Anti-Defamation League's ***Hate Hurts: How Children Learn and Unlearn Prejudice***

> This guide is a handbook for adults and children. Confronting and conquering bias and encouraging appreciation for our differences are the primary themes of this thought-provoking book, which seeks to help us understand that hate hurts and offers us ways to eradicate it.
> New York: Scholastic Inc., 2000

NONVIOLENCE RESOURCES

STUDENT BIBLIOGRAPHY

TuTu, Archbishop Desmond
No Future Without Forgiveness
> In this powerful and educational accounting of the pioneering activities of the Truth and Reconciliation Commission in South Africa at the end of apartheid, Archibishop Desmond Tutu moves beyond platitudes and presents a bold spirituality that recognizes the horrors people can inflict upon one another, and yet bears witness to the possibility and power of reconciliation and healing in the most unspeakable human circumstances. With a clarity of pitch born out of decades of experience, Tutu shows readers how to move forward in forgiveness with honesty and compassion to build a newer and more humane world.

Trujillo, Michelle L
Why Can't We Talk?: What Teens Would Share if Parents Would Listen
> In this accessible, positive book, teens and parents will find much with which to identify. The format, which reveals a diverse group of teens talking about pertinent issues, allows the reader to relate and to learn in a way that reduces fear and invites the opportunity for enhanced communication.
> Deerfield Beach: Health Communications, Inc., 2000

Wathen, Cindy (Edited by), Ann McGregor (Compiled by) and Ballis, George Elfie (Photographs by)
Remembering Cesar: The Legacy of Cesar Chavez
> Forty-five first hand accounts of Cesar Chavez, leader of the United Farmworkers, who fought for dignity, wages and humane working conditions for migrant workers.
> Quill Driver Books/Word Dancer Press, Inc., 2003

MIDDLE SCHOOL

Alexander, Lloyd, et al.
The Big Book for Peace
> The wisdom of peace and the absurdity of fighting are demonstrated here by various authors and artists in different ways: funny stories, serious tales, poems, pictures and even a song.
> New York: Dutton Children's Books, 1990 (out of print, use library)

Bridges, Ruby
Through My Eyes
> On November 14, 1960, six year old Ruby Bridges, surrounded by Federal marshals, walked through a mob of screaming segregationists into her school. She was a pioneer in the movement to integrate schools and this is her story. The book includes quotes from other writers and photos of this historic and moving event.
> New York: Scholastic Press, 1999

Brill, Marlene Targ
Journey for Peace: the Story of Rigoberta Menchu
> This is the story of a true woman of courage. Rigoberta Menchu is the 1992 Nobel Peace Prize winner for her work in Guatemala, where she traveled through her country helping native people everywhere learn how to protect themselves and to fight for justice. In doing this work, she risked her life to help her people, through teaching principles of nonviolence.
> New York: Dutton, 1996

NONVIOLENCE RESOURCES

STUDENT BIBLIOGRAPHY

Cameron, Susan
Out of War: True Stories from the Frontlines of the Children's Movement for Peace in Colombia
Stories of nine members of the Colombian Children's Peace Movement, nominated three times for a Nobel Peace Prize. CPM organized a national children's referendum for peace.
Lindforth: Scholastic, Inc., 2001

Dadamo, Francesco
Iqbal
Pakistani youth escapes bonded labor in a carpet factory and becomes an activist and advocate on behalf of child laborers. His murder at 13 years old inspired an international movement on behalf of these children.
Burnside, Quimby Warehouse 2003

Gandhi, Arun
Legacy of Love, My Education in the Path of Nonviolence
A poignant collection of stories and reflections on Arun Gandhi's time with his grandfather, the man known to the world as the Mahatma.
New York: Orbis Books, 2002

Hamanaka, Sheila (Compiled by)
On the Wings of Peace
This book is dedicated to the memory of Hiroshima and Nagasaki. Poems, short stories and exquisite illustrations by 60 writers and artists speak out for Peace in a variety of ways inspiring and creative ways. Many cultures represented.
New York: Clarion Books, a Houghton Mifflin Company imprint, 1995

Kuklin, Susan
Iqbal Masih and the International Crusaders Against Child Labor
New York: Henry Holt & Company, 1998

Lowry, Lois
Gathering Blue
A disabled girl, dealing with loss, leads the reader on an exploration of creativity, community and values.
Boston: Houghton Mifflin Company, 2000

Markova, Dawn and Daphne Rose Kingma
Random Acts of Kindness
Get in action with these stories of random acts of kindness and the movement is inspired!
Berkeley: Conari Press, 1996

Murdock, Maureen
Spinning Inward: Using Guided Imagery with Children for Learning, Creativity and Relaxation
This is a resource for teachers that includes skills and techniques that can be used with children to practice deep listening and enhance relaxation and imagination.
Boston, Shambala Press, 1987

NONVIOLENCE RESOURCES

STUDENT BIBLIOGRAPHY

Peters, Julie Ann
Define 'Normal'

> In this novel, about a "normal" teenage girl, who volunteers to participate in a peer counseling program, learns things she wouldn't have expected when she is paired with a "punker, druggie, gang banger."
> Boston: Little, Brown and Company, 2000

Pinkney, Andrea Davis
Let It Shine: Stories of Black Women Freedom Fighters

> The ten women featured in this book let their lights shine on the darkness of discrimination. Included are stories about the challenges and triumphs of the battle for civil rights; about speaking out for what you believe, even when it feels like no one is listening.
> San Diego: Gulliver Books Harcourt, Inc., 2000

Severance, John B
Gandhi: Great Soul

> In his lifetime, Gandhi was a London trained lawyer, the founder of several newspapers, a civil rights activist and so much more. In this book, we come to know this man, who believed in patient, peaceful resistance; satyagraha—a combination of truth, love and firmness. His life changed the world.
> New York: Clarion Books, 1997 (out of print)

Strasser, Todd
Give a Boy a Gun

> This work of fiction is a call to stop the violence and explore the role of guns in the lives of teenagers. The story is told through the interweaving of the voices of students, teachers and the gunmen themselves.
> New York: Simon and Schuster Books for Young Readers, 2000

Uchida, Yoshiko
A Jar of Dreams

> This touching and very real story depicts in lively detail the life of a Japanese girl and her family, who survive with spirit and determination, through difficult times in California during the Depression.
> New York: Atheneum, 1981

Yolen, Jane
The Devil's Arithmetic

> A Jewish teenager experiences history in a novel way when she is suddenly transported to a Polish village during the Nazi era in 1942. She is the only one who "knows where they are taking us."
> New York: Puffin Books, 1990

NONVIOLENCE RESOURCES

NONVIOLENCE VIDEOS

The Fight in the Fields: Cesar Chavez and the Farmworkers' Struggle, © 1997

> Producer: Rick Tejada-Flores
> Distributed by: The Cinema Guild
> This film joins social history of the agricultural labor movement with a biographical portrait of Cesar Chavez. Chavez and the United Farmworkers inspired Chicano activism of the 1960s and 1970s and in the process touched the consciences of millions of Americans. Befriended by Robert Kennedy and attacked by the Teamsters, Chavez was the most important Latino leader in this country's history.
> 130 Madison Avenue
> Second Floor
> New York, NY 10016
> (212) 685-6242
> orders@cinemaguild.com

Frontline: A Class Divided, © 2003

> Director: William Peters
> Jane Elliot, an elementary school teacher addressed racism in her class by developing the "Blue eyes/Brown eyes" exercise that left a deep impression of the evils of prejudice and racism, and demonstrated that racism is a learned behavior. This is the story of the lesson and its lasting impact 30 years later.
> 1-877-PBS-SHOP, by faxing your order to (703) 739-8131
> (include item title and number and credit card information), or by mailing your order to:
> PBS Video
> PO Box 751089
> Charlotte, NC 28275

A Force More Powerful: A Century of Nonviolent Conflict

> Producer: Steve York
> This six-part series tells one of the century's most important and least-known stories—how nonviolent power overcame oppression and authoritarian rule. In South Africa in 1907, Mohandas Gandhi led Indian immigrants in a nonviolent fight for rights denied them by white rulers. The power that Gandhi pioneered has been used by underdogs on every continent and in every decade of the 20th century, to fight for their rights and freedom. Reviewing a century often called the most violent in human history, this powerful series is the story of millions who chose to battle the forces of brutality with nonviolent weapons—and won.
> Contact: Films for the Humanities and Sciences
> P.O. Box 2053
> Princeton, New Jersey 08543
> (800) 257-5126
> www.films.com

Long Night's Journey Into Day: South Africa's Search for Truth and Reconciliation, © 2000

> Producer/Director: Frances Reid, Director: Deborah Hoffmann
> For over forty years, South Africa was governed by the most notorious form of racial domination since Nazi Germany. When it finally collapsed, those who had enforced apartheid's rule wanted amnesty for their crimes. Their victims wanted justice. As a compromise, the Truth and Reconciliation Commission (TRC) was formed. As it investigated the crimes of apartheid, the Commission brought together victims and perpetrators to relive South Africa's brutal history. By revealing the past instead of burying it, the TRC hoped to pave the way to a peaceful future.

NONVIOLENCE RESOURCES

NONVIOLENCE VIDEOS

Long Night's Journey Into Day: South Africa's Search for Truth and Reconciliation, © 2000, *continued*

  Contact: California Newsreel

  149 Ninth St., #420

  San Francisco, CA 94103

  (415) 621-6196

  www.newsreel.org

Soldiers of Peace: A Children's Crusade, © 1999

  By Kyra Thompson, Kathy Eldon, Lydia Smith

  Produced by CNN

  In October 1996, the children of Colombia staged a special election known as the Children's Mandate for Peace and Rights. Some 2.7 million children voted for the rights they considered most important. The overwhelming majority voted for the rights to life and peace. Subsequently, the Colombian Children's Peace Movement was nominated for a Nobel Peace Prize.

  Study Guide is available on the Web site (www.turnerlearning.com/cnn/soldiers/index.html)

  Purchase tapes for $10 plus $3.50 for shipping:

  Common Peace, Center for the Advancement of Nonviolence

  1223 Wilshire Blvd., #472, Santa Monica, CA 90403

The Treewoman

  A Film by Zin Rideaux

  A wonderful 30 minute film about Julia Butterfly Hill who lived in 200 foot tall redwood tree from December 10, 1997 through December 19, 1999 to protest the cutting of old growth forests.

  (310) 823-4790

Tutu and Franklin: A Journey Towards Peace

  Producer: Wisdom Works

  The Journey begins with the historic first encounter between Nobel Peace Prize winner Archbishop Desmond Tutu and renowned historian and Presidential Medal of Freedom recipient Dr. John Hope Franklin. On Goree Island, the infamous former slave port off the coast of Senegal, the two meet and discover surprising truths about their personal lives, and their nations' struggles for racial peace. Joined by an international, interracial group of 21 high school students, together they engage in a series of unusually candid encounters on race and begin an emotional journey towards racial reconciliation. Challenged by Tutu and Franklin, the teenagers directly, and at times emotionally, share their personal stories, and confront their ethnic stereotypes about each other.

  www.pbs.org/journeytopeace

  (202) 638-7870 to order a viewer's guide, community dialogue and teacher's guide

Twilight: Los Angeles

  By Anna Deavere Smith

  Adapted from Anna Deavere Smith's searing one-woman play, captures the tumultuous and challenging moment in America's race relations. It interweaves Smith's performance with documentary footage to examine this event from the point of view of diverse characters (developed from her interviews with Los Angeles residents).

  www.pbs.org/wnet/stageonscreen/twilight/index.html

  (800) 344-3337 to order from PBS Video

NONVIOLENCE RESOURCES

NONVIOLENCE VIDEOS

The Shadow of Hate: A History of Intolerance in America, Teaching Tolerance © 1995

> By Charles Guggenheim
>
> A project of the Southern Poverty Law Center
>
> 400 Washington Avenue
>
> Montgomery, AL 36104
>
> (334) 264-0286
>
> www.splcenter.org
>
> The *Shadow of Hate* chronicles episodes of intolerance throughout U.S. history—from the plights of Quakers in colonial New England to the 1991 riots in Crown Heights, Brooklyn, N.Y.
>
> The kit includes:
>
>> The award-winning film, "Shadow of Hate," available in VHS format
>>
>> The highly acclaimed text, "Us and Them"
>>
>> Teachers' guide

A Time for Justice: America's Civil Rights Movement, © 1995 Teaching Tolerance

> By Charles Guggenheim
>
> A project of the Southern Poverty Law Center
>
> 400 Washington Avenue
>
> Montgomery, AL 36104
>
> (334) 264-0286
>
> www.splcenter.org
>
> In 1954, a movement spread across the South that would change America forever. It was a nonviolent revolution that, ironically, claimed the lives of many people who died for the cause of equal rights. This documentary is an overview of the pivotal events of the Civil Rights movement. It is also a tribute to the men and women who rode where they weren't supposed to ride; walked where they weren't supposed to walk; sat where they weren't supposed to sit; and who stood their ground until they won their freedom. Historical footage and interviews recreate the crises in Montgomery, Little Rock, Birmingham and Selma—struggles that were rewarded when the Voting Rights Act was passed.

GLOSSARY OF NAMES AND TERMS

Jane Addams

Founder of the social settlement Hull-House in Chicago, activist for peace, women's suffrage, the rights of workers, children and the poor. She received the Nobel Peace Prize for her writing, her settlement work, and her international efforts for world peace.

AIDS Quilt

The AIDS Memorial Quilt is a poignant memorial, a powerful tool for prevention education and the largest ongoing community arts project in the world. Each of the more than 44,000 colorful panels in the Quilt memorializes the life of a person lost to AIDS.

Amnesty International

A worldwide movement of people who campaign for internationally recognized human rights. AI acts to prevent and end grave abuses of the rights to physical and mental integrity, freedom of conscience and expression, and freedom from discrimination, within the context of its work to promote all human rights.

Johnny Appleseed

John Chapman, 17th century American folk hero, who traveled all over the country planting small apple orchards and telling tall tales.

A.T. Ariyaratne

Founder of the largest non-governmental, nonviolent People's Development Movement in Sri Lanka, active in thousands of villages in all regions of the country, working for peace, development and human dignity.

Ann Bigelow

Founder of the Women's Anti-Slavery Society and a part of the Underground Railroad.

Billings, Montana

A town whose citizens came together in 1993 to fight hate crimes and in the process learned of the incredible power of people united for peace and tolerance.

Boycotts

An effective nonviolent strategy to generate social change by refusing to purchase goods and services from a targeted community. Examples: Montgomery Bus Boycott, Indian boycott against British textiles during struggle for independence, the United Farm Workers' Grape Boycott, and Port Elizabeth boycott in South Africa during apartheid.

Ruby Bridges

The first African-American child to desegregate an elementary school, in 1960. The first year, no other students attended.

Mary J. Blige

Overcame drugs, alcohol and depression to become a successful and mature soul and hip hop recording star.

Deitrich Bonhoeffer

German Protestant minister and pacifist who opposed Hitler and participated in an attempt to assassinate Hitler.

Gwendolyn Brooks

The first African American woman to earn a Pulitzer prize. She is credited with many other awards for her poetry and prose, inspiring many and being a voice for African American community.

George Washington Carver

Ex-slave who transformed the southern economy by diversifying crops (peanuts, sweet potatoes and soybeans) and developing over 300 products; also known as the "man who talked to flowers."

Cesar Chavez

Labor organizer, advocate for nonviolent social change, immigrant and migrant worker rights; founder of the United Farm Workers Union; posthumously awarded the Presidential Medal of Freedom.

GLOSSARY OF NAMES AND TERMS

Chipko "Tree Hugger" Movement

Indian movement that emerged in response to deforestation and destruction of land by corporations. Dissenters "hugged" trees to keep them from being cut down. This movement for ecological security uses culture in the expressions of reistance, and nurtures people's relationship with nature.

Clamshell Alliance

The first, organized antinuclear group to engage in direct nonviolent protest in the U.S.; Members occupied the power plant in Seabrook, New Hampshire and inspired a nationwide movement.

Colombian Children's Peace Movement

Mobilized 2.7 million children in a children's peace referendum in war-torn Columbia. As a result, ten million Colombian adults along with the children went out to vote for peace in Colombia with no violence during the voting.

Compassionate Listening Project

Dedicated to empowering individuals to heal polarization and build bridges between people, communities and nations in conflict.

Delano, Plan of

A 1996 call to action by Mexican American field workers, to justify the decision to walk 340 miles from Delano to Sacramento in support of the Delano Grape Strike and to declare that Mexican American workers would seek social justice by claiming their "God-given rights as human beings."

Dorothy Day

Cofounder of the Catholic worker movement, Catholic worker newspaper and "Houses of Hospitality" for the poor and homeless. She chose "voluntary poverty" and advocated for peace and disarmament, women's rights, and a more humane society.

Doctors Without Borders

Nobel Peace Laureates who deliver emergency aid to victims of armed conflict, epidemics, and natural and man-made disasters, and to others who lack health care due to social or geographical isolation.

Frederick Douglass

Former slave, abolitionist, writer and advisor to President Lincoln. He worked to amend the Constitution and assure African Americans rights after slavery.

Earth Day

On the first Earth Day, April 20, 1970, twenty million Americans participated in demonstrations. It changed the way people all over the world think about the Earth and our responsibility toward it.

Eugene Debs

Indiana statesman, labor organizer, ran for President five times. His last candidacy occurred while he was in prison for violating the Espionage Act by speaking against the war during World War I.

Albert Einstein

One of the most brilliant mathematical physicists of the century who is responsible for the famous "Theory of Relativity," among other invaluable discoveries. Einstein was also a philosopher, moralist, and a passionate advocate for freedom, peace and disarmament.

Jane Elliott

An elementary school teacher addressed racism in her class by developing the "Blue eyes/Brown eyes" exercise that left a deep impression on the evils of prejudice and racism, and demonstrated that racism is a learned behavior.

GLOSSARY OF NAMES AND TERMS

Daniel Ellsberg
Whistleblower who released the Pentagon Papers to the New York Times, revealing that Americans had been misled about Vietnam. Federal charges against him were dropped when it was discovered that the government had burglarized his offices to discredit him.

Victor Frankel
Holocaust survivor, developer of existential psychotherapy and author of *Man's Search for Meaning;* "Everything can be taken away from man but one thing, [the ability] to choose one's attitude in a given set of circumstances, to choose one's own way."

Freedom Summer 1964
During the summer of 1964, thousands of civil rights activists descended on Mississippi and other Southern states to try to end the long-time political disenfranchisement of African Americans in the region.

Paulo Freire
Brazilian adult educator, who worked to empower peasants in Brazil through an approach to literacy known as "popular education," articulated in his book, *Pedagogy of the Oppressed.*

Global Witness
Investigative organization, working to expose the link between natural resource exploitation and human rights abuses, operateing in areas where environmentally destructive trade is funding conflict or human rights violations.

Goldman Environmental Prize
The Goldman Environmental Prize is given each year to six environmental heroes—one from each of six continental regions: Africa, Asia, Europe, Island Nations, North America and South/Central America.

Fannie Lou Hamer
A share cropper who became one of the heroes of the Civil Rights Movement, an organizer for voter registration in Mississippi despite great personal cost. Hamer helped establish the Mississippi Freedom Democratic Party and will be remembered as one of the great inspirational singers of the Movement.

Vincent Harding
An author, scholar, activist and professor of religion and social transformation; Senior academic consultant to the award-winning PBS television series, Eyes on the Prize; Co-chairperson of the Veterans of Hope Project: A Center for the Study of Religion and Democratic Renewal.

Vaclav Havel
A playwright and dissident leader, who worked to reinstate democracy in Czechoslovakia. He became president of the Czech and Slovak Republic after the "Velvet Revolution" ended Communist rule.

Stephen Hawking
British theoretical physicist who suffers from Lou Gehrig's disease, explores the laws governing the universe.

Highlander Research and Education Center
A popular education and research center for grassroots organizing and leadership development; historically involved in the Southern Labor Movement, the Civil Rights Movement, and Appalachian people's movement.

Julia Butterfly Hill
A young woman who spent two years living in a California Coast Redwood tree to protect it and the surrounding forest from destruction. She has since spent her time working to make people more aware and grateful for their surrounding natural environment.

Hiroshima Maidens
Twenty-five heroic women disfigured by the bombing of Hiroshima who were brought to the U.S. by private citizens for reconstructive surgery.

GLOSSARY OF NAMES AND TERMS

Jose Ramos-Horta

Nobel Peace Laureate, advocate for the right to self determination for the people of East Timor; leading human rights advocate.

Dolores Huerta

In 1962 along with Cesar Chavez, she co-founded what would become the United Farm Workers Union (UFW). She continues to organize and lobby for worker, immigrant and women's rights.

International Peace Bridges

Peace Brigades International (PBI) is a non-governmental organization (NGO) which protects human rights and promotes nonviolent transformation of conflicts. They send teams of volunteers into areas of repression and conflict because their presence, backed by a support network, helps deter violence.

Ervin "Magic" Johnson, Jr.

Concluded his basketball career, in which he earned five NBA championship rings, after contracting HIV. He went on to become a major philanthropist and investor in neglected communities.

Helen Keller

Miraculously triumphed over blindness and deafness, one of the most intriguing and inspiring figures of our time. Graduated from Radcliff College 1904 and authored 13 books and countless articles. She was a pacifist, socialist, suffragette and lecturer.

Kenya Greenbelt Movement

Initiated by Wangari Maathai and the National Council of Women in Kenya; organizes women to plant trees and become more skilled farmers, addresses deforestation issues, the relationships between food, population, and energy and develops leadership among women.

Sister Chan Khong

Co-founder of the School of Youth for Social Service (along with Thich Nhat Hanh), which grew to an organization of over 10,000 young people organizing medical, educational, and agricultural facilities in rural Vietnam, and rebuilding villages destroyed by the war. Author of *Learning True Love*.

Rev. James Lawson, Jr.

Called the "foremost non-violent theorist in the world" by Dr. Martin Luther King, Jr., he trained the students who initiated the Nashville sit-ins, and became leaders in the Civil Rights movement. Rev. Lawson continues to be an advocate for disarmament, labor rights, human rights, peace and justice, and human dignity.

Le Chambon Sur Lignon

A village in France that hid 5,000 Jews during World War II. The leaders were known as "responsables"—those who are accountable.

Letter from a Birmingham Jail

A letter written by Martin Luther King, Jr. in his jail cell in 1963, in response to criticism from white ministers to his nonviolent campaign. One of the key documents explaining the nonviolent Civil Rights Movement of the 60s.

The Listening Project

A heart-centered approach to community organizing, grassroots empowerment and creative conflict management. Listening Projects employ deep listening to break down walls and barriers that separate and dis-empower people and communities.

Nelson Mandela

Former president of the African National Congress and political prisoner or Robben Island for 27 years. First president of post-apartheid South Africa, Nobel Peace Laureate for his tireless fight against racism and oppression, healing reconciliation, and peace.

GLOSSARY OF NAMES AND TERMS

Million Man March
A grass-roots mobilization across African American religious and class lines for a day of "unity, brotherhood, atonement and reconciliation" for black men and a call to up-lift African American communities.

Mothers of Plaza del Mayo
A group of women who became a symbol of human rights, activism and courage. Dressed in black, they have been demonstrating for years every Thursday at 3:30 in the afternoon, in the famous Plaza de Mayo in Buenos Aires, demanding to know the fates of their of sons and daughters who disappeared under political repression.

Margaret Mead
Was committed to anthropology as a human science and to learning from other cultures. As a public figure, she spoke out on and wrote about race relations, gender roles, culture, environmental justice, education, health and nutrition, child rearing, and self-empowerment within communities.

Muhammad Ali
Heavyweight boxing champion three times, who was stripped of his title when he refused to serve in the military during the Vietnam War due to his religious beliefs; his conviction was overturned by the Supreme Court.

Robert Muller
Former Assistant Secretary-General of the United Nations. Mr. Muller has spent the last 30 years working for world peace through the UN and has written more than 4000 *Ideas and Dreams For a Better World.*

Martin Neimoeller
Was a pastor who spent over seven years in a concentration camp for his sermons that were against Hitler and his Nazi regime. Martin Neimoeller also spoke out against nuclear weapons.

Nobel Peace Prize
Annual prize given to those who, during the preceding year, "shall have conferred the greatest benefit on mankind" and that one part be given to the person who "shall have done the most or the best work for fraternity between nations, for the abolition or reduction of standing armies and for the holding and promotion of peace congresses."

Rosa Parks
Who, by refusing to give up her seat on the bus to a Caucasian passenger, sparked the Montgomery Bus Boycott, launched the Montgomery Improvement Association and the rise of Dr. Martin Luther King, Jr. Her experiences as a member of the NAACP and student of Highlander School, prepared her for nonviolent civil disobedience.

Alice Paul
Stood up to Congress and the President of the United States and fought for an acceptance of the idea then men and women were equal. She dedicated her life to the single cause of securing equal rights for all women.

Peace Pilgrim
A woman who vowed to "remain a wanderer until mankind has learned the way of peace, walking until given shelter and fasting until given food." In the course of her 28 year pilgrimage she touched the hearts, minds, and lives of thousands of individuals all across North America.

Popular Education
An educational tool used to raise people's understanding of how their personal experiences are linked with larger social problems and empower them to create change.

Princess Diana
Princess of Wales who became a crusader for the International Campaign to ban landmines.

Christopher Reeve
Actor, director, activist who, after a spinal cord injury left him paralyzed, created a new life as a champion for people with disabilities. Author of *Still Me.*

GLOSSARY OF NAMES AND TERMS

Paul Robeson
Athlete, actor, singer, Rhodes Scholar and activist for human rights, labor rights and peace for people around the world. Blacklisted. Autobiography: *Here I Stand.*

Eleanor Roosevelt
First Lady, champion of human rights, women's issues, civil rights, farmers, and the poor and marginalized; responsible for development of the Universal Declaration of Human Rights.

Aung San Suu Kyi
Burmese Nobel Peace Laureate, who through a great deal of self sacrifice and perseverance, has worked to end repression and open her country to democracy.

Vandana Shiva
Indian environmental activist and founder of Research Foundation for Science, Technology and Ecology. Vandana works to increase ecological, cultural, economic, political security through what she calls "Earth Democracy."

Oscar Arias Sanchez
Former president of Costa Rica, winner of the 1987 Nobel Peace Prize for championing such issues as human development, democracy, and demilitarization, and initiating peace negotiations in Central America.

U.S. Sanctuary Movement
A group of sixty U.S. churches that have helped Salvadorian and Guatemalan immigrants enter the United states through a modern day underground railroad. The group then helps immigrants find a home and work.

Senal Sarihan
Mother, lawyer, feminist, wife, playwright, director, teacher, union organizer, editor, advocate, leader. A prominent human rights lawyer, Sarihan has made strengthening civil society and promoting women's rights in Turkey the focus of her work.

Sarvodaya Movement
See A.T. Ariyaratne

Anna Deavere Smith
As an actor, playwright and teacher, Anna Deavere Smith. Her one woman show, *Twilight: Los Angeles, 1992*, examined the civil unrest after the Rodney King verdict through characters representing diverse experiences and points of view.

South African Truth and Reconciliation Commission
Created to address atrocities committed by all sides under Apartheid. It grants amnesty to those who confess their roles in full and can prove that their actions served some political motive.

Anne Sullivan
The 21 year old "Teacher" who taught blind and deaf Helen Keller to communicate with the world; Helen Keller's companion until Anne died.

Mother Teresa
Winner of the Nobel Peace Prize and founder of the order of Missionaries of Charity. She and her community devoted their lives to the poor, the sick, and the dying who were shunned by the greater society.

Harriet Tubman
A "conductor" on the Underground Railroad, this escaped slave brought more than 300 slaves to freedom.

Bishop Desmond Tutu
Nobel Peace Laureate, first African General Secretary of the South African Council of Churches, anti-apartheid activist, head of the South African Truth and Reconciliation Commission, and a pivotal leader for justice and reconciliation in South Africa.

GLOSSARY OF NAMES AND TERMS

Uwa Indians

A nation of 8,000 Indigenous people in Colombia, being evicted off their sacred land by oil companies. They threatened to commit mass suicide rather than leave their land.

Underground Railroad

A network of aid and support to help American slaves successfully escape to the North and freedom before Emancipation. Many people, whites and blacks, illegally assisted slaves to freedom.

United Farm Workers Union

Founded by Cesar Chavez to advocate for the rights of migrant farm workers. Under his leadership, the Union successfully launched its grape boycott and won the right to unionize, challenged the use of pesticides, increased wages and improved working conditions.

United Students Against Sweatshops

An international student movement of campuses and individual students fighting for sweatshop free labor conditions and workers' rights.

Lech Walesa

In December 1990, in a general ballot Walesa was elected President of the Republic of Poland. He led the nonviolent Solidarity movement and helped establish free and independent Poland.

Oprah Winfrey

Survived poverty, rape and molestation to become one the most powerful television personalities in TV history as well as a film producer, actress, business mogul and philanthropist.

Witness For Peace

Supports peace, justice and sustainable economies in the Americas. Witness for Peace works through education, travel and personal experience to spread their message of nonviolent change.

REFERENCES

Creighton, A. & Kivel, P. (1992)
Helping Teens Stop Violence (2nd ed.). Alameda, CA: Hunter House.

Creighton, A., & Kivel, P. (2002)
Liberation theory and practice. In Cantor, R. & Oakland Men's Project (eds.) *Days of respect: Organizing a school-wide violence prevention program* (pp. 16-17). Alameda, CA: Hunter House

Fellowship of Reconciliation (1999)
The challenge of the next century. *Fellowship Magazine*, May-June, no page.

Fellowship of Reconciliation (1999)
What is a culture of nonviolence? *Fellowship Magazine*, May-June, no page.

Frankl, V.E. (1963)
Man's Search For Meaning. New York: Simon and Schuster, Washington Square Press.

Gandhi, A. (1996)
Blunders of the World. Retrieved January 2004, from *www.gandhiinstitute.org/Library/ArunGandhi.cfm*

Hymes, J. L., Jr. (1996)
The Columbia World Of Quotations (1996) Retrieved March 30, 2005, from www.bartleby.com/66/

Heider, J.
The Tao Of Leadership: Leadership Strategies For A New Age. Atlanta, GA: Humanics Limited, Bantam.

LaFayette, B., Jr., & Jehnsen, D. C. (1995)
The briefing booklet: *An Orientation To The Kingian Nonviolence Conflict Reconciliation.* Galena, Ohio: International Human Rights Reports (IHRR).

Murdock, M. (1987)
Spinning Inward: Guided Imagery For Children. Boston: Shambhala Press

Nobel Peace Laureates (1999)
For the children of the world. *Fellowship Magazine*, May- June, no page number.

United Nations General Assembly (1999)
International decade for a culture of peace and nonviolence for the children of the world. (2001-2010), *Fellowship Magazine*, May-June, no page number.

Zimmerman, F. & Coyle, V. (1996)
The Way Of Council. Las Vegas, NV: Bramble Press.

ABOUT THE AUTHORS

CARL STUDNA

Eisha Mason is a visionary, author, gifted speaker, and innovative educator dedicated to advancing creative nonviolence as a universal tool for personal and social transformation.

Through her leadership as the Executive Director of Common Peace, Center for the Advancement of Nonviolence from 1997 through 2005, Eisha guided the development of an exponentially growing community of peace educators and activists. She has gained a reputation as a trusted, effective communicator who inspires hope and facilitates understanding and action.

Eisha is the author of *Mapping Violence – Creating Change*, a transformation curriculum for teens, and is co-author of the *64 Ways to Practice Nonviolence, Curriculum and Resource Guide*. She hosts *The Morning Review* on KPFK radio, where she engages people in dialogue about peace, justice and non-violent social change. Some of her most noted guests have been Nobel Peace Laureate Thich Nhat Hanh, Dr. Vincent Harding and Robert Muller.

Eisha has a track record of more than 20 years working with youth in a variety of settings. Whether as the director of OASIS, a program for teens in foster care, or as a consultant to the National Conference of Community and Justice (NCCJ) and National Family Life and Education Center, Eisha combines compassion, creativity and accountability in her approach.

A sought after speaker, seminar leader and world traveler, Eisha received her bachelor's degree from the University of Maryland and her master's in applied psychology from the University of Santa Monica. She serves on the faculty of both the Agape International Spiritual Center and Holmes Institute. She may be contacted at eishamason@sbcglobal.net.

TALI STEIN

Peggy Dobreer is an inspired speaker, teacher, poet, and advocate for nonviolence in our schools and communities.

She served as the Education Director and member of the Executive Committee of Common Peace, Center for the Advancement of Nonviolence, from its inception in 1997 through 2004 and is co-author of *64 Ways to Practice Nonviolence, Curriculum and Resource Guide*.

Peggy's exceptional gifts and talents as an experiential educator, performance artist, writer and craftsman make her a dynamic creative force in the development and implementation of these Common Peace educational materials and programs. She skillfully facilitates multiple-intelligence learning whether working with incarcerated youth or with students and teachers in public and private school settings, including The John Wohlman School, Crossroads School for Arts and Sciences, The Country School, and numerous independent learning programs, university master classes and international conferences.

A graduate of Whittier College and a Religious Science Practitioner, Peggy is a recurring guest speaker at the First Unitarian Church of Los Angeles, hosts *A Horse of Another Color* poetry in West LA and works at Loyola Marymount University. Her poetry has been widely anthologized including: *The Voices from Leimert Park: Volume II, Wordwright's Magazine, Literary Angles: The Second Poetic Diversity Anthology, The Tamaphyr Mountain Press Irregular*, and *Cracked Pavement and Plastic Trees: Our Gifts to Future Generations*. Peggy can be reached at adhocink@yahoo.com.

Inquiries for both authors may be directed to: Common Peace, Center for the Advancement of Nonviolence, 1223 Wilshire Blvd., #472, Los Angeles, California 90403, (323) 931-9125, www.nonviolenceworks.com, email: centernv@sbcglobal.net.